LANCASHIRE MEMORIES

BITS AND BOBBINS FROM BOLTON

BY

Sylvia Luke Bibby

WRITTEN IN 2015 – 2016

MAP OF LANCASHIRE ENGLAND

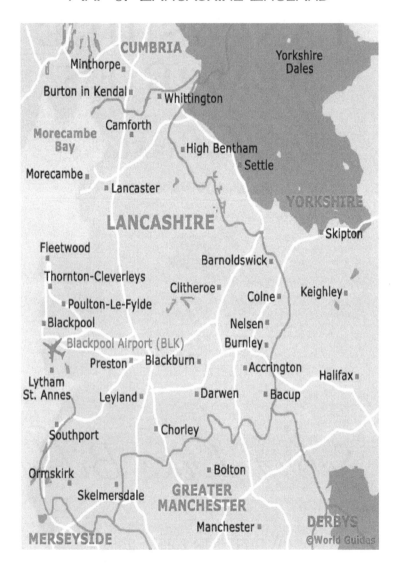

Author's Email: sylviabibby301@gmail.com

Printed in the United States of America.

Genre: memoir, historical, inspirational

Author: Sylvia Luke, Bibby 1937 -

Title: LANCASHIRE MEMORIES, Bits and Bobbins from Bolton

Cover Design: Marguerite Patricia Gilner

ISBN: 9798425036841

Library of Congress Control Number: 2022903931

CHAPTERS

FORWARD AND DEDICATION

I wrote these memories in 2015. I had been working since 2011 on a little handwritten book for each of my family. I began them when my health took a severe downturn in 2011, and it seemed that my time might be short. I slowly got better, but I had filled the books, and I was still living! I realized there were many more memories I could have shared, so I felt the urge to set them down in more detail. I thought I would only revisit the World War Two years, but as I wrote, I had a desire to write all sorts of things about life as I lived it in Lancashire in 1937, until I left for college in London in 1955. It was a different world then. I had some trepidation as I contemplated going back down this particular Memory Lane, but it was enjoyable in the end! It gave me a new appreciation for the opportunities of my life, the people in it who had helped me, and for my Lancashire roots. I had often only thought of Bolton as somewhere to leave, not to go to, but from where I am on my journey now, I see so much value in it all and all the gifts it gave me. I also developed profound gratitude for those in my family who have gone before me. Their struggles were hard, and I admired the way they persevered and was in awe of so many of the life stories I have come to know. I am very grateful for it all.

I dedicate this to my wonderful daughters, Kay Antoinette and Amanda Jane, two beautiful, creative, and courageous women. I hope that these memories will interest my four grandsons and great-grandchildren, Owen, Emma Jane, and Harrison. They are the lights of our lives here on earth. We never forget our precious great-grandson Luke Phillip, who watches over us all from heaven. I pray you will all hold fast to your roots, do your part in the story of our family, stay close to each other, and I hope this writing links you to your English heritage. I love you all!

Our Two Daughters, Kay & Amanda
A Joy and a Blessing!

A photo of Me at Age Three

Chapter One

ARRIVAL - 1937

W hen I was born, I was up in the top corner of the room, looking down on the scene. That has always been my earliest memory! I was aware that I was in a tiny row house on Shaw Street. Bolton, Lancashire, and looking down at that very sparse little bedroom, the bed tousled by the unrelenting and unstoppable process of childbirth, and at my mother-to-be who was trying to be stoic but fraying at the edges. A well-built midwife was in attendance, and I had this distinct impression of floating above this scene accompanied by somebody else. I don't know if any negotations went on; the receiving spot in the world that I appeared destined for didn't look too prosperous or encouraging at first glance. If I did have any last-minute objections, they were overruled and rejected. It was made clear to me that in April 1937, Bolton, Lancashire wasn't such an unfavorable spot; after all, it could have been Russia, Germany, China, Japan, or any number of places poised on the brink of World War II chaos. Looking back now, I'm glad no one listened to my misgivings and swapped my assignment.

So I entered this mortal coil! "Eeh, look at the big limbs on this child!" said the midwife as she dealt with my entry. "Big Limbs" were going to be a feature in my young years, much to my chagrin. In the Lancashire view back then, "big limbs" was a compliment of sorts indicating a thriving child, but to me, it always made me feel like some big galumphing elephant! I guess this was the seed of life-long regret that I wasn't small and dainty! Ah well.

So I arrived in Bolton, a big town in the industrial North of England, and in 1937 it was very industrial with around 240 cotton mills going full belt in all directions, with chimney stacks smoking and spreading clouds of lint in the areas around them like some plague of Egypt. There was also an unbecoming coat of black grime from the industry over everything and from the coal fires that everyone had. Have you heard about "dark satanic mills?" We had them in spades. Before I was two years old, we moved from Shaw Street to live in Cecilia Street, Great Lever. This street was one of a line of six. The last one, Weston Street, was definitely in bad repair in those days. The dilapidated houses showed absolute poverty, age, neglect, and an air of general malaise. There were cracked windows, peeling paint, chipped doorsteps, and front doors that opened directly onto the street. More traffic came down Weston Street, contributing to the dust and grime. It also faced a mill now being used for other purposes. Our Cecilia Street was the next one to Weston and marginally better. The streets improved one by one until you hit Parkfield Rd at the top, which was viewed as a significant cut above and somewhere to strive for. Still, though our street was second to last in the desirable stakes, most of the ladies resolutely mopped their front steps outside every week and patiently donkey stoned them to highlight the edges in white. As I grew older, I often got this job and knelt there with an old sack for a pad. I would frequently sigh, as it seemed that soot fell faster than I could mop or scrub.

Cecilia Street had a huge working cotton mill at the bottom end and a narrow ginnel-type lane at the top end. This ginnel ran along with the Mill Lodge that was full of water. I never knew what purpose the water served. Railway sleepers formed a fence, but it couldn't keep us kids out. Even threatened by a good hiding if we went near the Lodge, we would squeeze our way in there and climb the raised bank to survey the water vista of the flat square lodge. The Lodge was about as near to nature as we got for a water feature, For our flowers, we had rosebay willowherb, coltsfoot, and dandelions.

Our street was cobbled down the middle and had flag pavement stones on the sides. One of our happiest pursuits in summer was squatting down in the middle and popping the tar bubbles that surrounded the cobblestones. Mind you, with English weather, that wasn't a regular event! It's odd what you find to do when you don't have many toys. The houses were simple row houses, and the front doors in Cecilia Street opened onto the street with just a doorstep in front of it. It was two up two down, and you entered the front room, which had a grate and fireplace with a black leaded cooking oven. The other room was the kitchen with a small table and assorted chairs, a gas stove, one small food cabinet, and a sink. Of course, there was a clothes dryer, a rack that pulled up on a rope to the ceiling on which clothes took up residence till they dried after washing day, which was on Monday. The back door led out to a small backyard; at the end of that was the outside loo. Let me hasten to add there was no inside loo. It was torture to have to go out there first thing in the freezing morning. I resolutely refused to use the only other alternative. Upstairs there were two small bedrooms, one front and one back. In the middle was a tiny box room, and in later years, it would become the bathroom for whoever owned the house.

Across the street from us lived a lady we called

Auntie Winnie. She had no children but liked kids and their company. She was always welcoming if you turned up, and would chat and give you a biscuit, a cup of tea, and listen to what you had to say. Being a child who had a LOT to say, I often found myself less than welcome in my own house, enough being enough! Endless gabbing will wear down even the most devoted of parents. Auntie Winnie's was a haven. Wearing her ever-present floral wraparound overall (all ladies wore a wraparound back then), she would put the kettle on, listen happily, and always have time. Uncle Frank was large, similarly easygoing, and he sat and read his paper if he was in and didn't pay too much attention. They weren't biological relatives to any of us; we all just called them Auntie and Uncle in response to their affectionate interest. We didn't know then that Uncle Frank would spend so much time as a Japanese prisoner in a war camp in World War II and return to Cecilia Street after the war weighing about 90 lbs. and in terrible shape. It's good we don't know our futures. Cecilia Street had a cast of characters. We were # 40. Several doors down in #28 was my friend Jane. We both had red hair, but there the similarity ended. She was nicely rounded, had gorgeous ringlets, and always looked neat. I was always gawky (how could I not be with those "big limbs"). My red hair fell over my face as I was constantly losing my hair slide, and I was never tidy, with my blouse out, stain on the skirt, scarred knees, you get the picture. Jane and I were friends despite all this. Across from us lived a family called Pilkington. I remember their youngest was Raymond, and he was very skinny and didn't look to be thriving too well. My only memory now is of us happily popping tar bubbles together and his mother erupting suddenly from her front door and dragging him off with baleful glances at me for leading him   astray. Down the street lived an elderly couple with a daughter who was a six-year-old child in a young woman's body. She wanted to play with us and often did. I look back now and wonder at the burden these parents shouldered in caring for her and keeping her safe. In later years men would arrive in cars, and she would always climb in and be driven off, then eventually delivered back. Horrible. We didn't understand what was going on, but it was worrying for her parents. Even though she was twice our size, she played with us, always submissive but happy to be with us all. It's heartbreaking as I look back now, and I often wonder what became of her when her parents died.

Life wasn't easy for our parent's generation. Still, we were all tied together by National Events and formed a community full of people getting on with life and trying to do their best while enjoying the times when we could celebrate together.

Chapter Two

WAR MEMORIES

1939 TO 1945

I was young when the war started and eight when it ended, but I have many memories. I'll do my best to share them and want to be as faithful as I can to what I do remember.

Now we had moved to Richelieu Street, the next one up in the hierarchy of streets. The Bolton Evening News came every day. I began to notice that a quiet gloom and focus would descend in the house after its arrival, and football news and local diversions were no longer the order of the day. Sitting at the kitchen table, there would be a lot of head shaking and muttering from my father, and it soon seeped into my mind that something was seriously amiss. Then on Sunday, September 3rd, 1939, a Special Edition of the Bolton

Evening News arrived in the house, and the world outside our streets crashed into our world with a vengeance. The paper, which cost one penny, bore a large headline "BRITAIN AT WAR WITH GERMANY." Also noted was that France's ultimatum to Germany expired at five pm, and Mr. Churchill was named First Lord of the Admiralty. Smaller headlines announced "Germany Claimed Capture of Historic Polish Town" and "Hitler Going to the Eastern Front." So at 11 am on this momentous day, Britain declared war on Germany. King George VI was to broadcast to the Empire at six pm, and another item was "Commons Cheers for the Premier." A copy of the Ultimatum issued from Downing Street was on the front page. In every town, sandbags were being filled, and work was reported to be going on "apace." Lorries bearing sand were rolling, most buses weren't running, there were few cars to be seen, and the streets in the nation were mostly empty. Suddenly, the realization set in that the time for uncertainty, indecision, and waiting for deadlines had passed. The dye was well and truly cast, so sandbags became very important, and complying with lighting restrictions was now a serious matter. More casual and cavalier attitudes faded away as reality sank in.

It was also noted on the front page that 240,000 men were registered for service in June and not all had been called on but now training was needed and action was imperative. Mr. Hore Belisha reassured everyone that before sending any men under 20 years out of the country he would explain to the House the circumstances that made that necessary and he hoped that youth of 18 years would not have to be called. Sadly this was a hope soon to be dashed. I can imagine the sinking hearts of many mothers and wives as they read these things. Other front-page items were that the St. Leger race meeting was canceled, warnings were given to vessels entering the Firth of Forth, and the King and Queen were listening together to the news in their private rooms at the Palace. The paper went on to note amazing scenes taking place in Whitehall; people with flags and gas masks were milling about, some sporting German steel helmets, (leftover from the first world war no doubt). Apparently after initial quiet when the deadline passed, the crowds began cheering and growing in size. Downing Street and Whitehall began to fill up with people waving flags, cheering, and excitement erupting after the first period of awed silence.

So, the war began. During the long years, I remember the sirens sounding the alarm; a sound that raises goosebumps and fills me with alarm and agitation even today. Later would come the All Clear. We had a terrible air-raid shelter in our tiny backyard. It wasn't properly finished, was wet and cold and full of fat worms and earwigs who could care less what the humans were up to. Our enthusiasm for going into that shelter died pretty quickly and mostly I was hustled out of my bed, quickly pushed into the storage space under the stairs on a hastily erected board in there that was hard and so uncomfortable. Night after night, listening to the sound of strident and ominous sirens, and being deposited under the stairs, this night routine occurred. I think the trouble with sleeping that I have had in my life might have started with all this confusion, tension, and disruption. It all took place in Lancashire weather too, so often it has bitterly cold and damp. Several times that I can remember, Air Raid wardens came round to all the houses in our street and those surrounding, and bullied us all outside in our nightclothes, clutching blankets, and, of course, our gas masks. Once outside with everyone else we were herded down the street in the pitch dark due to the "blackout", down to the cotton mill at the bottom of the street. We all filed into the basement and sat on whatever was available, a barrel, a plank, a cotton bale, or mostly the floor. German planes flew over us on their way to Manchester and Salford, cities doomed by their docks and industries to be hot targets. Even today I can remember and hear again the sound of the German plane engines droning as they passed overhead, wave after wave, and the stillness in the basement as we clutched blankets and each other and anxiously listened to them. If any bombs hadn't rained down on Salford or Manchester, there we were on their route home as it were, so leftovers could be dropped on us. Great relief came when the planes were gone and the All Clear began to wail. We would gather ourselves up and tramp wearily back from the mill through the dark street and into our homes, exhausted! Usually, the penultimate British reaction to all calamity would happen and you would hear "Let's put the kettle on and have a cup of tea" after which we would fall into our beds to make the most of what was left of the night.

Gas masks had been issued to everyone before the actual outbreak of war. They were in a container with a strap and were supposed to accompany us everywhere. We all had to practice wearing them and would sit there in our rubber snouts trying to get the straps right. At school antics with the gas masks must have driven the teachers crazy. The school had a large underground air-raid shelter taking up most of the playground. On several occasions after the siren began the alarm all over the town, we were quickly lined up and rushed outside to go into the shelter. It was dark in there, with a rough floor, planks to sit on, and as children, 5 years to 11 years were involved, little kids had to sit on the laps of bigger kids. All of us were instructed to put on the dreaded masks and it took no time at all for the boys to begin making terrible farting sounds with their masks. Loud shouts from frazzled teachers would ensue threatening the offenders with a good hiding! Times were different then! It took kids about five seconds after being given their gas masks to figure out it could make these horrible noises! I picture us now, sitting in rows on the planks that gave splinters, looking like a cross between a Dickensian scene from Oliver Twist and little aliens with black snouts, most of the male aliens making horrible noises! Time was also enlivened by shrieks of horror as alarmed spiders would appear and earwigs would run up the walls. A worm or two also enlivened the procedures. We were town kids and reacted badly and hysterically to the slightest invasion from the insect world. Sometimes we sang. Try THAT in a gas mask! All in all, it was a great relief when the All Clear would sound, and back inside we would go after packing away the gas masks in their cases. My eldest cousin Irene put all sorts of things in her gas mask case. I remember seeing in hers a tiny lipstick and a small blue owl that held a little bottle of cologne called Evening in Paris. That was later in the war after she had discovered Americans were not far away from Bolton and off she would go to Blackpool to see "Yanks." I hadn't the slightest idea at that time who THEY were, and now I am one!

My school was St Simon and St Jude in Great Lever, Bolton, just a short walk from our house. It was an old building even when I started at five years old, and was a Church of England school that I remember so fondly and with so much appreciation for the education and start in life it gave to me. In the School's 50th Anniversary Book, this War Time note was included and gives an insight into what was happening in an ordinary school as they coped with the war and its ramifications.

"During the 1939-1945 War period, considerable difficulty was experienced by teachers and scholars alike. Air Raid precautions made heavy demands all over town. In 1938 our school was selected as a building suitable for conversion and used as a gas decontamination center to meet the possibility of gas warfare. Water storage tanks were installed in the building and baths of various kinds were provided. Emergency doorways were made and the cloakrooms were specially protected so they might be used as shelters. Air Raid Wardens were for a long time, accommodated in the schools. Later the children's playground facing Forester Hill Rd was excavated and underground shelters were provided for the safety of teachers and scholars, in 1940 classes were being held in the homes of a number of parishioners. When hostilities ended, the school had to be put back in order, a task which had to be spread out over several years."

I remember the wartime as pretty dreary with bitterly cold winters that continued after the war. Food was so scarce and even though the friends who had one of the allotments would share the fruits and vegetables they grew, it was usually large bunches of rhubarb. To this day I'm not fond of rhubarb! Too many bowls of unsweetened rhubarb will do that to you.

Mind you, I ate it then, as I, and everyone else, would eat anything offered because we were always so hungry. How our mothers kept us fed on the meager rations just amazes me now. I know a marrow bone would produce pea broth that featured large on our menus. As a Scottish friend would say "Let's go crazy today, put another pea in the broth!" Dried eggs were pretty terrible, horse meat appeared a couple of times, but in general protein was scarce and also involved a long queue at the butcher's shop. Queues were just a fact of life and we queued up for everything. Discipline and queue etiquette were rigidly held to. Later in life when I traveled to other countries where it was every man for himself, I was aghast! Life would have been unbearable if that same approach happened in England during the war! Another memory is that daily my Mother would put me in front of her, and out would come the Government issued cod liver oil and concentrated orange juice. I loved the orange juice but hated the cod liver oil which she always wisely dosed me with first. Protestations, grimaces, and groans were of no use at all. To my mother, if Winston Churchill said children had to have cod liver oil, that was it, they were getting it, no arguments.

Winston Churchill figured large in our lives. I remember my mother, father, and myself, (my brother came along later in 1944), sitting around the kitchen table, listening to the BBC "pip pip pip" before the news came on or to Big Ben chiming from our tiny decrepit wireless. These broadcasts were so important because they were our only contact with what was going on in a wider context. The daily news was pretty dreadful most of the time, but we gave rapt attention when Mr. Churchill spoke. He was the right man in the right place at the right time, and his powerful words were the glue that held us together and stiffened our resolve through terrible times. Now as I look back and read his words, I feel such deep gratitude to him. He was an amazing man and I have always known that it is thanks to him that I have had the opportunity to live the life I have been blessed to live. It all could so easily have gone in another direction too horrible to think about. How we loved to see the pictures of him striding about, even in the rubble of buildings, with his cigar and his fingers in the Vee for Victory sign. He was and still is my hero.

Then there was the blackout. All windows had to have black curtaining that showed not one chink of light and zealous Home Guards would go around banging on the door and yelling "Get that light covered" if there was the slightest chink. Also, none of the street lamps were ever lit and cars had to drive without their headlights. That wasn't such a problem around where I lived, as there were no cars, but if any did pass by, it was in the pitch dark and at about three miles an hour! Walking to church or anywhere in the pitch dark was an adventure. I remember walking into a lamppost one night and getting an awesome bruise.

Eventually, the war ended and men who had disappeared five years ago to who knows where appeared home again. My Uncle had been in Egypt for four and a half years where he was a very welcome unknown source who sent boxes of Turkish Delight to break the monotony of our wartime diet. Its cloying sweetness made me feel a bit sick as I didn't pace myself, but it was such a joy to get it. He arrived home suddenly after all those years away. Uncle Frank came home a little later when VJ day came, but he was a shadow of his former self, 90 lbs., and sunk in interior pain and terrible memories of the Japanese Prison Camp where he spent so many years. Post War he was playing lawn bowls with friends at a hotel nearby called the Brooklyn. A couple of businessmen brought a Japanese colleague to lunch there and they came out to look out at the grounds. There was consternation when it was realized that Uncle Frank had gone into a strange intent state and had begun following the Japanese visitor around and things were very obviously going to have a bad end. His friends hustled him off home with some difficulty but saved an international incident. Eventually, and unbelievably, the war years ended though they had seemed endless.

ANOTHER POSE OF ME AT AGE THREE

CELEBRATING THE WEDDING OF

PRINCESS ELIZABETH IN 1947

Chapter Three

STREET PARTIES

So finally, VE Day arrived! Victory in Europe Day! As I write this, the 70th anniversary of this momentous day has just been celebrated. VE Day brought such a release of joy and relief and for one glorious day, smiles, waves, and gatherings took place. Of course, Cecilia Street, led by the intrepid and indomitable Auntie Winnie, held a Street Party, the first one I experienced. All of us kids were dazzled by the very idea. A party? We couldn't wait as the aproned ladies in their headscarves got together to plan this extravaganza. The day finally arrived, and we poured out into the middle of the street to watch the preparations. From attics and under-bed storage, rather tatty lines of bunting emerged, no doubt leftover from World War I celebrations and wisely kept in case of need in the future. The world being what it is, the "in case " event happened sooner than anyone expected.

No matter, we had bunting! The houses on our street had a door and one window downstairs and one window upstairs. Reluctant men were recruited to string flags and bunting across the street from window to window. The men wrestled tables out of houses, and no matter how higgledy-piggledy the assortment, they were lined up unsteadily down the middle of the cobbled street. Chairs appeared, as did tablecloths of all shapes and sizes and in various stages of wear and tear. Soon, led by Auntie Winnie, each household's contribution to the feast was carried out and put on the tables. Wobbly jellies emerged from molds jiggling in jeweled tones and looking glorious. Blancmange, mostly a bilious pink, sat solidly on platters, shaking when moved. Mounds of bread and butter and sandwiches were added, known of course as "butties," mainly jam butties. My favorites were bacon butties, but they weren't available till well into the post-war era! During the war, many recipes appeared showing how to make something out of nothing. Many of these confections appeared at the party, contributed by the ladies who had saved coupons for just this occasion. Rock buns were favorites, and due to the shortage of eggs, they tended to be, like their name indicated, real jawbreakers. We loved them anyway. When it was all set out and ready, the whole street sat down together to feast and washed everything down with gallons of tea (of course!) We all waved flags, and once we had stuffed ourselves, we sang wartime songs. "Hang Out

Your Washing on the Siegfried Line" was one and another from World War I was "Goodbye Dolly Gray." This song was my grandmother's particular favorite, and I can still sing every word of it today. "It's a Long Way to Tipperary" and "Roll out the Barrel," "White Cliffs of Dover," "We'll Meet Again," one after another, we sang them all. This scene went on in countless streets all over our large town and the whole country, and it was terrific. Everyone forgot the pressure of war. Victory was the word of the day.

Sadly, the post-war years were to prove equally hard to endure, bitterly cold winters, still shortages of everything, a country full of ruined buildings, and not enough housing to go around. I can remember a visit to my Aunt Catherine in London and riding down Oxford Street on a bus seeing mainly bomb sites, the rubble of buildings, piles of bricks, and capsized roofs on both sides of the road. There were holes where buildings were obliterated, then suddenly a building that had survived it all, standing untouched. It was a daunting situation all over the country with much needing to be rebuilt. It was very depressing. There were times when people wistfully heard about the Marshall Plan for Europe and the rebuilding of Europe and Japan. There was no help for rebuilding for us. As victors, we had to pay off our lend-lease and debt to America, and recovery seemed so slow. But back to the street parties! Our next one was for Princess Elizabeth's wedding and Cecilia Street's party was visited by a reporter from the Bolton Evening News. As a result, a photograph of us appeared in the evening edition! Fame indeed! There we are, a line of children, Jane in a long dress and with her immaculate ringlets, me with my hair down (lost the hair slide again !) Jane had a flower chaplet on her curls and held a big wedding cake. Things had improved a bit in the ingredients department by then!

I'm so glad that this tradition of street parties has remained through the years. Though living abroad now, I love reading about the street parties for the Queen's Jubilees and other occasions, and just this last week, parties for the 70th anniversary of VE day!

CELEBRATING VE DAY

THE END OF WORLD WAR II IN 1945

Chapter Four

ST. SIMON AND ST. JUDE

When I was five years old, I went to St. Simon and St. Jude Church of England School in Great Lever, Bolton. I walked into Miss Battle's class for the first time in awe. Who knows how many of us there were, but later in life, when I taught in England briefly in the '60s, I had 46 five-year-old's in my class at one point, so odds are there were a lot of us back then! The class sizes were high, but we were different five-year-old's at that time; in general, we behaved. We were all deliciously horrified one morning at Register time when Neil's name was called, whereupon he boldly answered, "Here, Miss Battleship!" We were aghast and Miss Battle apoplectic. Miss Battle ordered a swift visit to the Headmistress for the cheeky monkey! Registers were important; each morning and afternoon, the first order of business was for the class names to be ceremoniously called out and answered smartly as elegant ticks were placed by each name, or the very rare X if not present. These registers were revered objects and had to be done in ink. When I became a teacher myself and had one of these Holy Grails, I lived in dread of blots and splotches or, heaven forbid, inaccuracies.

My memories of school in those days are that I loved it and took to it like a duck to water. I could already read, so that was a big help; however, I could NOT tell time, and when I was given the coveted job of going down the corridor to the next class to look through the window in the door at the clock and then come back and tell my teacher the time, well, horrors! I used to ask the teacher in the room with the clock what the time was, and then go back as if I had known it for myself! Surely, they knew I did this? Why did she pick me so often! I remember the old worn-out steps that took you to the upper level. They were well-worn as the building was built in 1901; many feet had clattered up and down those stairs. There were three pictures on the walls of the stairwell, one a picture of Jesus about three years old entitled Little Hands Outstretched to Bless, another one of Him kneeling in a garden surrounded by animals and birds underneath a blossoming tree, and the third was of a shepherd boy with lambs. I LOVED those pictures, and I was delighted about 40 years later to find them as postcards in a shop in Bolton. I had them framed, they still hang in my bedroom today and make me happy when I see them.

I remember Assemblies every morning and singing together gathered in the hall to begin the day. We also had Chorus as a lesson and learned so many songs, Barbara Allen, Men of Harlech, He Who Would Valiant Be, I Vow to Thee my Country, Jerusalem, Widdicombe Fair, and so many others.

The classrooms had high ceilings; the furniture was old. The desks had inkwell holes and I vividly remember the day ink was introduced to us. A pot of ink was slotted into the inkwell, pens were issued, all of which had horrible nibs. The splotching began in an atmosphere of palpable anxiety! I was horrified to make such a mess and got ink all over my hands and skirt, but a quick glance around reassured me that I wasn't the only one at all!

For Physical Education, we all stripped down in the classroom to our vests, panties, and underpants. Out we would be herded into the playground no matter what the weather. Lots of jumping, relay tag races, hopping, skipping, jumping ropes, and ball throwing ensued. Then suitably sweaty, we would be lined up and marched back in to pull our clothes on again. No one ever seemed to mind as it was just what happened. There was no time for modesty, or it never occurred to us. We were all in the same boat. Years later, when we lived in St Croix, I had a class of seven-year-olds in an American private school. I had zero experience of American schools or practices. One day I blithely had them strip off to their undies, and out we went to do some P.E. After the initial shock, the kids got on with it and didn't seem to mind, but that evening the headmaster received quite a few angry phone calls from outraged parents who were horrified about it! Lesson learned, never again! I must admit I was surprised that Americans, who in my mind were so free-spirited and informal, could be more prudish than English parents! I was astounded actually, not knowing what all the fuss was about, but suitably apologetic. I explained, and promised it would never happen again!

Back to my school, who can forget having to work money problems with pounds, shillings, pence, halfpennies, and farthings! Having to borrow and remember four farthings in a penny, two halfpennies in a penny, twelve pennies in a shilling, twenty shillings in a pound, and one sum could give you a real workout! In addition to all those, there were threepenny pieces known as threepenny bits, and half-crowns, having a value of two shillings and sixpence. Thank goodness they weren't in the sums!

Endless chanting of multiplication tables went on in every spare minute, whether sitting down or standing in line to go somewhere or waiting for something to happen. Daily we recited them over and over, and I have never forgotten them, that's for sure! It was like Korean brainwashing.

The church of St. Simon and St. Jude was right next to the school, and we would often go there as seasons progressed throughout the year. The Harvest Festival was significant, as it was everywhere, harking back to the rural roots of every area. We stood in the middle of this huge town with mills all around, a coal mine at the top of the main road, and though the harvest was not an experience in our lives, the Festival survived and was much anticipated. Days ahead, the church would be full of ladies at work. All the window embrasures were decorated with sheaves of wheat and elaborately braided loaves of bread. The volunteers placed autumn flowers and plants everywhere, and it all looked beautiful. At the Harvest Service, the school would gather in church with the congregation. Halfway through the service, everyone would process up to the altar steps with our spuds, cauliflowers, and huge bunches of the prolific and dreaded rhubarb if your Dad had an Allotment. We sang, "We Plow the Fields and Scatter, the good seed on the ground." We had never done any plowing or scattering but had seen the pictures! And so the year would move on to the Nativity Play at Christmas, the Carol Service with Nine Lessons, the Easter services with new hats, shoes, and a coat proudly worn if you were lucky, and family funds allowed. We would often have services to celebrate special national events, and the church would be packed with all the school children in front and parents and congregation filling up everywhere else. I loved it all. The music was of a high standard and blessed me every time I heard it. It all provided a framework to life, traditions, and a comforting structure that made me feel content and part of something good.

The 1944 Education Act opened up Higher Education to more children, so I was lucky to benefit from this. At ten years old, we entered the anticipated but somewhat dreaded 11 Plus year. More well-off kids had coaching; the rest of us had to rely on unguided native talent. You were to take this 11 Plus exam at the end of the year, and it would determine your future. Literally. A few coveted Grammar School slots would possibly open up the chance of university education. If you didn't get that there was Secondary School (I guess the name they gave it says it all). The next option was Technical School, where trades were taught. This exam was taken with deadly seriousness. Thankfully as my 11 plus year began, we had a new young teacher named Miss Margaret Walker. She was a product of new teacher training and proved to be a fantastic educator. We did all we were supposed to, reading, math, history, geography, spelling, mental arithmetic, scripture, general knowledge, and all the rest. We also got to write plays and stage them, learn Esperanto and all sorts of other amazing things. Despite some people's trepidation about a newfangled young teacher, my class went on to do exceptionally well in the 11 plus exam and amaze everybody. I was truly blessed to have Miss Walker. I count her as one of the angels that appeared to bring untold blessings, change and help throughout my life. It was such a relief when it was over, the pressure was off, and I had won a grammar school place and a town scholarship to Bolton School. Bolton School is one of the oldest schools in Lancashire, its origins traced back to 1516. It was an Independent School, not a State-Run school, and that year 40 scholarships were given to pupils from the town. I was blessed to receive one of them. Heady, and what an opportunity.

I loved my time at St. Simons. Assessing it now, I know it was an excellent start, a place of discovery, opening things up to me, a framework of traditions, and an introduction to new things. I will always be grateful and look back fondly. Thirty-five years later, when we were home on leave from the U.S. Virgin Islands, we went with my parents to St. Simons, which was now a Club that served meat pies, sausage rolls, and other goodies and had a bar full of different ales, spirits, a live band and so on. It felt strange sitting there in the room where I first entered school, aged five. It was all so changed. The building was there, but very different in layout and atmosphere. Happy memories, though, and I am so grateful for my years there and count myself lucky to have had that start to my education.

St. Simon and St. Jude Church

Chapter Five

CHURCH AS A CENTER OF LIFE

n addition to being my first school, St. Simon and St. Jude provided a natural center and focus in our lives. It wasn't only our church but a center for other activities. I was a Girl Guide until I was 16 years old and ended up as a Queen's Guide with an armful of badges. Miss Walker ran that with her usual aplomb and talent, and I loved it. I remember a treasure hunt we had where we all set off with a list of items to find and bring back. Number four on the list was "A Footprint" I lugged back a footprint of a man's size 12 shoe in a massive piece of soggy clay that oozed a very unappealing yellowy mud all over me. What was I thinking? Not one of my finest moments! We were meant to find a sparrow footprint or some such small manageable item! But no, here I came, staggering in with my enormous lump of oozing clay to the dismay of all and my humiliation when I realized how foolish that was.

St. Simon had an excellent choir. I joined as an alto though I had daydreams about turning into a sublime soprano! I had piano lessons from when I was eight years old, so reading music was a decided advantage. The choir was led by a fine organist and choirmaster, Mr. Harry Leyland, and the standard was high. We sang for the 10:30 am Matins every Sunday and the 6:00 pm Evensong. At the morning service, we sang an anthem in four parts, in addition to the hymns and psalms. Choir practice was long, businesslike, very serious, and held every week. Woe to giggling young sopranos, Mr. Leyland would brook no-nonsense, and in his hands, that baton would rap louder than you could ever imagine. Young or old snapped to attention. I loved all the opportunities to sing in the church choir, and as a child, we also had chorus at school all the time. It was all very satisfying, and a means to experience and touch the universal in life. We all took part in it, and it wasn't optional. Singing was part of our lives.

The choir had an annual picnic, and well do I remember lining up to get on the Charabanc, known as the Sharra, or the Coach, to sound more regal! Finally, all on the bus and settled, off we would go, usually to the seaside somewhere. The sea isn't far from anywhere you live in England, which is a huge plus. We would hardly be down the road a mile before out came the sandwiches and bottles of pale ale. On this occasion, we were off to Chester Zoo (not the sea), and we were all in merry spirits when we arrived. Our visit was considerably enlivened by a swan. We were walking along a path near the lake when suddenly, from the bushes erupted this swan in full outrage and battle cry, with wings flapping wildly, long neck outstretched, and the beak snapping alarmingly. It also made terrifying noises and charged right at us, singling out one unfortunate soprano who was rather a heavy set lady and not at all in physical condition for rapid flight. The swan sent us all scattering, but this poor woman was last seen galloping up the path, screaming loudly as she was being swan pecked! We had walked too close to the nest and alarmed a very angry swan mother! We did feel they should have had a warning sign!

After this excitement was over, we had a good day at the zoo, and then the bus took us to a fish and chip shop nearby, where we all received our food wrapped in a newspaper. Well doused with malt vinegar, it tasted so good! Those who could afford it got mushy peas as well, not too easy to manage sitting outside on a wooden bench but worth the struggle. When that was all eaten, we were back on the coach for the return journey to Bolton. We had one more stop to make at a pub on the way home for more beer and pale ale. An Englishman's capacity for downing large quantities of beer and ale was incredible in those days, and for all I know, it still is. Once everyone had slaked their thirst, we were back on the Coach again for the final leg home. Being a choir, we sang most of the way home, and they weren't hymns let me assure you! We finally arrived back at the schoolyard in a happy and inebriated cloud of fumes. With loud goodnights, all set off to walk their separate ways home, some more steadily than others. Another picnic over!

A huge event in parish life was "The Sermons." All the parish organizations walked around the parish boundaries once a year. Banners led the way for each group, and periodically, the procession would stop, and a Sermon would be delivered. In addition to the many people in the procession, the streets were lined with onlookers. It was a big event. The best thing about it for us children was a group formed for this event, called "The Singers". Children of seven to ten years old could take part. If you were in "The Singers," you had to turn up in a white dress, white socks, black shoes, and this being Lancashire and not the South of France, a warm white woolen shawl. White headdresses were provided by the church, and it was all very thrilling. The economic standing of each singer tended to be reflected in the quality of the dress or suit, but I must say every family seemed to come up trumps for this occasion. A month before the event, practices were held several days a week after school and they were very rigorous. I can remember us having to sing a phrase repeatedly because our enunciation wasn't good enough or we were taking a breath in the wrong place. When the day arrived, we gathered in a classroom and then filed out in pairs to join the procession in all our finery. Girls, all like little angels in white, the boys in dark suits. We felt wonderful, special, and so excited. The procession would begin, and it was a long one led by a brass band as most things were back then in Lancashire and Yorkshire. We walked around the Parish limits, which was quite a long way. The stops gave us a bit of a rest and time to fidget a little through the sermon. The choir in their robes sang hymns on the way, so did the Mothers Union, the Men's Group, and on and on, each organization behind its banner. Once all the parading was over and we arrived back at the church, we all filed in for the service. As singers, our moment finally came, and we were lined up on the altar steps and performed the songs we had labored over for all those weeks. Some children had been identified early on as not really contributing to the overall effect in the required manner, and they had been sternly instructed to just mouth the words without making a sound. The result of all this was heavenly music and of a good standard. We felt like little angels that day.

The Church held Sunday School every Sunday

morning, and the children would file out from church to the school just before the sermon. I remember being at services from when I was five, and one of my earliest memories is responding to the singing of the psalms, and it affected me greatly. Eventually, having been a student in the Sunday School, I became a teacher and got the job of playing the piano for the singing at the gathering that began the classes.

The Church had a large and active Mothers Union formed in 1901. At the outbreak of war in 1939, their meeting room was taken over by an emergency police station, and the ladies had to transfer to the Upper Billiards room. It sounds odd that the school building had an upper billiards room which must mean there was a lower one too, but that was the report in the anniversary booklet the church put out in later years. The Mothers Union had a beautiful banner, and I remember seeing it in pride of place in the church. It was also prominent in the Sermons Procession and any other outdoor events. They were a formidable group of older ladies, and you crossed them at your peril! They were the ones who provided ample refreshments at any function, and for their meat pies alone, I loved them all!

Other active groups in the parish were the Men's Sunday Class, The Girls Friendly Society, Boy Scouts, Cub Scouts, Brownies, Girl Guides, The Young Wives Association, the Parish Magazine Committee, a meeting place for men in the Church House, and a Men's Club. There were many sports too, such as a Church Football team, (of course !) which played in the Bolton Sunday School League. In the summer we had a cricket team. A tennis club lasted till 1930, with a net strung across the playground to make a court, not leaving much room around the edges.

My favorite Church activity was the Dramatic Society. I loved it. It was formed in 1909 and produced plays. The 1910 production of East Lynn even toured other church schools in the town. On New Year's Day 1910, the cast, carrying all their baggage and props, trudged through the snow to Walmsley Church School to present the play. What an effort and all on foot in bitterly cold weather. Eventually, our school added a new stage and fittings, and many productions ensued. In September 1940, the Farnworth Auxiliary Fire Service Amateur Society staged a Variety Show at our school to raise funds for the Red Cross. Our Dramatic Society produced a Passion play every Easter, but my abiding memory is of the Pantomimes staged every Christmas time. I loved them as a child, and I have a cherished memory of being chosen at age 16 to be the Principal Boy in "Jack and the Beanstalk", and another year to be Prince Charming in "Cinderella!" The Principal Boy part has many solos to sing. How could I be so stupid as to go off to the Bolton Wanderers match at home and proceed to shout my head off all afternoon, only realizing with a sinking feeling on the way home that my voice was nearly gone! Horrors! That night wasn't my best performance, but I made it somehow! It was fun being in those shows as there were many rehearsals, and it was good to be with everyone, young and old, working together to make it happen. Then opening night would come, and the curtain would swing back as the music began, and the performance would begin, always to a packed house!

All this, of course, was before television, electronic devices, and all the technology that was to come in later years. I'm glad it was all available so I could get out of the house! We had to make our own entertainment and thanks to previous generations, the traditions were in place. We could join in or not. Most people in the parish did join in, and it was a true center of social life as well as spiritual life. I feel it enriched my life and blessed me.

St. Simon and St. Jude Church
Wedding of Sylvia and Norman

Chapter Six

THE CHURCH DANCES

On the 50th anniversary of the Parish 1901-1951, a magazine was produced and had this to say about Dances. "Dancing can hardly be classified as a sports activity, but it has been a most popular favorite during the winter months for many years. Prior to 1914, dancing was not considered a fitting form of enjoyment in a Sunday School. and for a long time, it was prohibited by our first vicar. The 1914-1918 War brought many changes and it was during that period that it was agreed that "Dancing may be allowed in the School on Saturday evenings under the strict supervision of one or both of the Church Wardens." The early Dance Bands were composed of a piano, violin, and cello, the players being drawn from our own scholars. A few years elapsed before Drums and any form of percussion instruments could be introduced. Almost continuously since that time, Dancing has formed a large part of the Saturday evening entertainment in the school. Despite the complete change which has taken place in the presentation of the Dances compared with the early days, "it is a form of entertainment that shows no signs of waning."

Well, all I can say is that the dances were great! Before I was old enough to be let loose at the large Palais de Danse in the town center, we always had the dances at church to go to, and even my father was hard-pressed to come up with a good reason to forbid me to go. Believe me, he tried! I soon learned the Quick-Step, the Foxtrot (not very well), and the Waltz. All of us had to give up and sit on the sidelines and watch the Tango when the band struck that up; none of us had a clue how to do it. All except for one couple who showed off terribly by swooping and vamping all over the place, and shades of early churchwardens going apoplectic with horror was easy to imagine. Nobody dared to have a go at the Tango, sensing instinctively that an amateur Tango could be disastrously embarrassing. The one and only Tango couple took it very seriously! The Tango was an ever-present part of any church dance back then, but unlike Argentinians, us Lancashire folk didn't have much of a clue!

The dance program interspersed "Old Time Dances" with the "Modern Ones." I loved the stately

Valeta, enjoyed the Military Two-Step, and once in a while we would have The Gay Gordons. We didn't have that dance too often, as the Gay Gordons could swiftly deteriorate into all kinds of mayhem, fueled by the bottled beer and ale being consumed steadily by thirsty dancers. The drinks had the name "Refreshments," which gave a kind of refined legitimacy, but no doubt about it, just like a football match, things got wilder when the alcohol level rose! The Gay Gordons is very boisterous and strenuous, and something about it seemed to cut loose some wild Viking blood in us Northerners. Normally sedate people would be hurtling around, getting redder, working up a sweat, laughing hysterically, especially when ending up going the wrong way or cannoning into people! It was fun, though, and it wasn't uncommon for it to end with a collapsed heap of dancers on the floor.

People dressed up as much as they could afford to for the dances. Many women brought their dancing shoes, usually silver or gold color, transported in a special shoe bag, so the cloakroom, already crammed with macs, brollies, and coats, had a shelf for outer shoes and boots. I could only dream of one-day having dancing shoes, but had to manage in my one pair of shoes, which were always what my mother referred to as SENSIBLE! (Sigh) I desperately longed for fancier shoes, and while on this topic, I also longed for a red coat, but that was never to be either! My mother was a "Money Manager of Next to Nothing" of the first order, and extras were not common! In any case, as she often told me, "Red doesn't suit redheads." All of this explains why the first coat I was able to buy for myself was, of course, red!

The dances always had an "interval, "when refreshments were served. Huge pots and urns of tea were brewed. No respectable English function ever happened without tables filled with cups, saucers, and copious amounts of tea. There were meat pies, meat, and potato pies, pasties, sausage rolls, and sandwiches of various kinds all set out by the Mothers Union ladies, who, when the locusts had descended, and crumbs remained, had the job of endlessly washing up. Entrance to the dances cost One Shilling and Sixpence, and I think refreshments were included! About 18 cents for a great night out!

The Last Waltz would eventually be called, and one desperately hoped that the right boy would ask you for that. It rarely happened. The band would then begin packing up, probably just as well, as they had been consuming bottles of ale most of the night in between tunes, and the music had begun to sound a bit haphazard! In a cloud of hazy cigarette smoke, chairs were stacked, the kitchen cleaned, and all would don their boots, wellingtons, warm coats, and off we would go with most ladies clutching their dancing shoe bags and their brollies. Looking back, I loved these dances! Mind you, that's not surprising, any event with a meat and potato pie involved is always a winner to me.

As I have looked back on writing this, I am so glad I got to have all these activities growing up. There were no TVs, video games, smartphones, iPads, computers, etc. People were happy getting together doing things and interacting with each other. It was self-made entertainment and very enjoyable. Post War life in England was hard. I remember such frigid cold winters back then with not much money about, strict rationing and living frugally, and never really as much to eat as you would have liked. Life at St Simon's was welcome because everybody knew everybody, and the traditions and events playing out year by year gave a structure and framework to our lives, and it was a good thing.

The Parishioners at St. Simon and St. Jude Church were human beings, so no use presenting a whitewashed picture of Lancashire churchgoers behaving like angels all the time and living out their faith in exemplary fashion. Oh no, where does that ever happen? Like everywhere else, we had our share of power struggles in the Mother's Union, Men's Club, etc. We sometimes had an ornery over proud churchwarden. We even had a Vicar and choir member scandal; it even made the dreaded national newspaper the News of the World. Hello? Remember, it's human beings who were in action here, living out their lives, and to me, there was nothing abnormal about these ups and downs as it was just life as it always is. Despite that peripheral human nonsense, there was a solid core of faith, caring, and goodness. It provided so much to enrich our lives, and I'll always be grateful.

This flow of church life fitted into the national life, which we were in touch with through the BBC, the radio, and the newspapers. We were one people then, one nation, survivors of a terrible war held together by grit, determination, and also by cups of tea, of course. The Royal family was loved and appreciated because we had gone through it together. The National Calendar of events also gave a feeling of belonging, a framework. Poppy Day was in November, and the two-minute silence over the whole country began as Big Ben in London chimed 11 o'clock. The King, Queen, and others stood in silence at the Cenotaph in Whitehall, but all over the country at War Memorials, others stood, and the whole country was silent and still for that two minutes. We remembered them. Then there was Guy Fawkes Day, November 5th, the Opening of Parliament, and so many other events that bound us all together. I am always grateful that that was my experience.

Chapter Seven

LANCASHIRE CHRISTMAS

So what do I remember about Christmas in Bolton? First that my father, no matter how "skint" he was, wanted to give us a "good" Christmas. It was so important to him. His childhood had involved the early death of his father, Thomas William Luke, from tuberculosis when my father was twelve. Pawnshops, in which his only boots would often find a temporary home, and other deprivations that came from his mother's struggles after being left a widow with four children under twelve, were difficult memories. He began work in the cotton mills when twelve years old. He had a burning memory of having to go for Christmas dinners provided by charities, and it always pained him to think of it. From all this emerged his wish to "have a good Christmas" no matter what, and we were the beneficiaries.

Our small tree would go up the week before. It

would have looked so much better if I hadn't gone upstairs as a three-year-old and, while looking into everything, found the hidden box of precious ornaments! I had hit the jackpot and played with them in such delight. Oh, the colors, the sparkle, the beauty! Oh, joy! Of course, when my mother found me sitting in the shards a little later, that meant that future trees would be a lot plainer. Money for such extras as ornaments was so hard to come by in those days. I think they had been a gift to my mother in the first place.

Christmas Day, we could hear church bells ringing as we woke up. My father would go down first and build up the coal fire, and there would be a stocking, a regular sock put to good use, not a fancy Christmas one. At the bottom of the toe would be a piece of coal for good luck, a tangerine (only ever seen at Christmas in our house,) a Christmas cracker, some nuts (also annual visitors to our diet!) Usually, there would be two or three large Brazil nuts, Walnuts, and some tiny hard ones, Hazelnuts, I think. All needed a hammer to be wielded; it was a lot of hard work for the revealed small contents, but they were a rare treat, so every morsel counted. I usually got a Film Fun Annual, Beano Annual, and a doll. After my brother came along, there would be a mechanical toy for him and other good things. That was pretty much it, but it seemed like a treasure trove to us, and we were happy. Later in the day, we would walk two streets over to my Grandmother Halstead's house in Melville Street. Each street seemed to rise in hierarchy back then, with each one up from Weston Street a little more prosperous till you hit Parkwood Rd, definitely a cut above. Walking into her house, the smell of roast chicken just hit you. The chicken was a once-a-year meal back then, in our family and most others. We enjoyed sage and onion stuffing, Brussels sprouts, roast potatoes and gravy followed by Sherry trifle, mince pies, and later the Christmas Cake that my mother had made. She always put little charms in it, with each one wrapped in a tiny twist of paper. If you got one of the little silver coin pieces, the old threepenny piece, this meant you would get money in the year following. The little horseshoe foretold good luck ahead for you. A tiny plastic baby was one charm no one seemed to want all that much. A small crown also bode well, and there were other charms.

"Spirits" would have been bought from the off-license for the day. Always a small bottle of whiskey (for medicinal purposes, according to my grandmother,) a small bottle of gin, and bottles of beer. Imbibing these soon increased the air of relaxation after we had eaten. My Uncle Albert was a gifted syncopated pianist with a vast repertoire, so we would end up singing and shouting out our requests. The day would draw to a close. Reading this over, it does all sound pretty idyllic, a jolly good time and all that, but guess what folks? This was a family, and the word that goes with that so easily is dysfunctional. We were pretty typical in that respect, and dysfunction flourished. There were tensions. My Grandmother played her two daughters, Ellen and Muriel, off against each other and seemed to enjoy any trouble she managed to cause. In general, she took a dim view of my Grandfather Wilfred too, so he came in for quite a few choice comments. After being married, my father was never the same after fracturing his skull while diving at the swimming baths. He could not be relied on to stay serene, tactful, quiet, or kind at these gatherings. Auntie Muriel was pretty good at passive aggression. My mother often seethed with pent-up emotion she found hard to express. You can imagine how it all went! But that's all part of a family gathering, right? Hey, it was Christmas. We had had a great feast, not to mention "the spirits," and it would be all back to normal the next day.

The next day was Boxing Day which is supposedly called that from the days when the entire household staff was presented with their Christmas present from the gentry they worked for. Presumably, it was in a box. Gentry were not thick on the ground where I lived and household staff in every house I knew consisted of Mum, but the name lived on and still does today. Mince pies and sherry had a prominent place on Boxing Day, and it would also be chicken soup time, using the picked clean carcass from our Christmas chicken. I can't tell you how prized that chicken was in those days. It was a once-a-year meal for us. Lamb or a small piece of beef were the cheaper meats. Nowadays, you need a second mortgage to buy either of those, and chicken is everywhere all the time! Times change! But back to Boxing Day, it was the day the Pantomimes opened. These traditional theatrical extravaganzas were just incredible. It's an art form all its own with unique traditions and customs. Titles included such delights as "Puss in Boots," "Cinderella," "Jack and the Beanstalk," "Aladdin " and more. The role of the Prince or the hero was played by a young woman, preferably with good legs. I played Principal Boy in two pantomimes put on at St. Simons when I was older. Not saying I had good legs, mind you (remember "Eeh, she 'as sturdy limbs!"); however, they must have been good enough to get me the part. I still fondly remember my green satin short shorts, worn, as custom required, to show lots of leg (sturdy or not!) A white long-sleeved shirt and a green satin waistcoat top completed the picture. With high heels and lots of makeup, I was Jack in "Jack and the Beanstalk" and loved it! The leading lady in pantomimes is always in sparkly full-skirted chiffon things and preferably has long curly hair. We thought nothing of a girl dressed as a boy wooing and singing to a curly-haired girly girl! It's just how Panto was and had been for centuries. Then, of course, there is always a Dame in every Panto. This part, such as Widow Twanky in Aladdin, was always played by a man, usually played by the top comedians of the day in the professional productions, and in amateur ones by someone who thought he was a comedian. They were a source of a lot of raunchy humor (think Benny Hill-type innuendo!) There was always a villain and lots of audience participation. All in all, there was a relatively thin storyline based on fairy tales embellished by lots of singing, dancing, and clowning around. There were many sequins, satin, and other finery and always a glittering Grand Finale. I only remembered going to one professional pantomime and loved it. I'm so glad they still survive, though I do wonder how a modern-day panto would be.

Other Christmas memories include carol singing. We did go around tormenting our neighbors with terrible renditions of "Good King Wenceslas" and other favorites. The boys always had their own words to substitute for the traditional ones; hopefully, nobody noticed their ribaldry and sniggers as us earnest ones sang the right words and tried to drown them out.

Going to town was a treat. Lots to see, and at the outdoor market, sprigs of holly were available from large piles brought in from the country waiting to be cut up into affordable sprigs. We could never afford mistletoe. It was always costly, and not too much of it was available. In our house, the decorations consisted mainly of colored paper cut into strips and painstakingly pasted up to make chains. The paste was made from ordinary flour and water and could be lumpy and unreliable. We would usually start pestering to start making them in September if allowed, but no way, Mother was resistant to all whines. Eventually, the day would come, and we would sit and make yards and yards of paper chains, rough and ready as they might be. Once festooned everywhere, draped from the center light and around the sides of the walls, they transformed the room and made us very happy. The tradition was that all decorations had to be down by January 6th, the Epiphany, or remain until Easter. Ours were always down well before the 6th, mainly because the paste didn't hold up that well. I never saw a house that still had them up, but that was the saying, and I guess it made sure there would be no arguing about it being time to dismantle Christmas.

The other Christmas events were the Nativity Plays. Every church and school had one acted out by the children. There was great competition to be Mary or Joseph, Angels, Wise Men, the Innkeeper or his wife, but not so much interest in being a shepherd. I'll never forget one school play, five or six rather small disheveled shepherds in long robes entered from the back of the hall arriving at the stairs at the side of the stage. They climbed up, and the last child in the group started climbing but unfortunately climbed into his long robe ending up in a huddled ball at the top end of his robe, totally immobilized and needing rescue. It was so hard not to laugh aloud, but as he was so mortified, it was necessary to stifle that and act as if nothing untoward had happened!

So, the Christmas season would end, carols would be retired till the following year, robes and wings were packed away and stored in school cupboards. Trees were dismantled and returned to the top of the wardrobe with the ornaments, withered holly would go into the dustbin with the somewhat tattered paper chains, and all too soon, Christmas was over.

CHRISTMAS IN BOLTON IN THE 1940S

Chapter Eight

THE TOWN CENTER

Bolton was a large town when I was born and is even bigger now. It began as a small village and vestiges of this older way of life still exist. There is a little green near the church, and nearby is the oldest building in town, a tiny pub called The Olde Man and Scythe. This irregular medieval building has black and white features, old beams, tiny windows, and a very ancient door. Across the road from it is Walshes Pasty Shop, another tiny ancient building, dating from the 16th century. The town grew because cotton mills and other industries were built, and workers were needed. People in the countryside needed work, so the eighteenth century saw them flock to where the work was. The Mill Owners became incredibly rich; the workers had a living but didn't become rich. However, the Mill Owners did use some of their riches to build a Town Center adorned with beautiful buildings. The Town Hall, with its soaring spire, the Crescent curving around it at the rear, all gave and continue to provide a solid sense of place and the feeling that it belonged to everyone, and that included me! When completed, it was opened by Edward, Prince of Wales. The Town Hall had grand steps flanked by two magnificent lions and was a great setting when the larger world visited. I remember the visit of King George VI just after the war was over (yes, the one in the movie "The King's Speech"), and of course, his wife Queen Elizabeth came with him. Huge crowds were delighted as the royal car pulled up to the Town Hall. They exited gracefully, waved to us all, and then ascended the flight of steps up to the large raised platform area at the top, waved again, and then disappeared through the large glass doors and into the Hall to be greeted by the Mayor of Bolton. This visit had a HUGE place in our rather lackluster family history. Ellen Halstead, my grandmother (yes, the one who liked medicinal whiskey,) was on duty that day at the Luncheon Banquet. She and her friend Cissy Yates were first-rate waitresses and were called in for the top jobs on the rare occasion that one came along! Clad in black with a white lace-trimmed apron and cap, Ellen stood with Cissy behind the two grand chairs set at the long banquet table for the Royal Couple. Cissy served the King, and Ellen served Her Majesty the Queen. They pulled out the chairs, helped to seat them comfortably, then zoomed off to begin the service of many courses. They were the personal waitresses for the King and Queen. At one point, the Queen's fur stole, which was draped over the back of her chair, slipped to the floor. Ellen sprang into action, picking it up and handing it to Her Majesty, and then helped to settle it more securely. Ellen was rewarded with a huge smile from the Queen, who said, "Thank you very much!" This whole event was a story told and retold countless times, and we all basked in the secondhand glory of my grandmother serving the King and Queen and actually being spoken to! An extra detail never forgotten in the telling was that the Queen had taken a minute portion of peas, apparently not caring for them too much. Either that or perhaps experience had taught her that peas were not too cooperative at public functions, all too often disinclined to stay on one's fork. It was lovely for Cissy and Ellen that their waitress career had this high point. They were also called in to serve General Bernard Montgomery when he visited Bolton as part of his "after the war " tour of the large towns. Unfortunately, he couldn't live up to the royal grandeur at all and wasn't a star feature in the stories of their Glory Days! I remember being in the crowd in the Town Hall Square on those two occasions. General Montgomery arrived, got out of his car, and it was a surprise that he was such a small but jaunty figure. He was a quick-moving person who looked full of energy even from afar. He was received with cheers; after all, El Alamein had been such an essential part of the war and a welcome victory. He had gone on to a distinguished career throughout the rest of the war and served us and his country well, though he seemed to have acquired a reputation for being rather difficult. With all his service, I think he can be forgiven for that.

The Town Hall stood in the large square with grand attractive buildings built on three sides. One housed the Co-op. We were there often. Just off the square was a store called Whittakers, much respected, very posh, and pleasant to visit. I remember the bills were written for your purchase, then put into a capsule container with the money, slotted into a tube, then off it would go through the suction channels ending up in the upstairs area somewhere to be processed. Eventually, with a whoosh, the tube would arrive back with your change and receipt. Shopping was a lengthy process in those days but pretty fascinating! I remember that Whittakers had a lift (elevator), the first one I ever rode in as they were rare. The store was definitely posh, and we rarely bought anything there. We would just go to stroll about as if we were going to buy all sorts of things, but we would leave and end up on the market!

Going to town was a big thing and a taste of something more than our streets, tiny houses, and the corner shop. It felt good to have these large buildings such as the Art Gallery, the Central Library (which was huge and awesome), the Aquarium, the stone lions, and the steps. Every child had to sit on the lions and climb the steps when young or just play galloping up and down them. Lancashire ladies back then mostly wore macintoshes for their shopping trips (no reason to wonder why); it rained or drizzled a lot in the North of England. The ladies also wore headscarves and carried wicker baskets or some other sort of shopping bag. You avoided buying too much heavy stuff at once as it had to be carried to the bus stop, onto the bus, and then off the bus to your house. That alone puts paid to any bulk shopping. The Town Center was big and enjoyable. A great bus service got you there easily, and if money was tight, we walked there and just rode one way back. So thank you, rich mill owners.

THE TOWN IN LANCASHIRE ENGLAND

Chapter Nine

THE MARKETS

have fond memories of the markets in Bolton. A charter to have a market was given on December 14th, 1251 by King Henry III, a Plantagenet king. In 1253 Bolton became a market town thanks to another charter from the Earl of Derby and on January 14th, 1253 a market was held and seems to have gone on from strength to strength ever since. My favorite market was the Indoor Market. The Market Hall was built in 1854 and was and is a wonderful Victorian building with a huge high ceiling and pleasing architecture. It was a favorite destination for me and my mother. We would walk to town, (a good long walk it was too,) then go to the Market Hall. There were shops all around the four walls and free-standing stalls filling up the center of the space, and sold food and produce of every kind, fish, meat, baked goods, confectionery, pots, pans, household wares, linens, material, fancy goods, toys, gift items, and so many other things. It was all a delight for the eyes and so good to be out of the all too frequent rain. Once our shopping was done we would go to a teeny tiny cafe that was tucked close to one of the entrances. It seated about six people at a time, tops, and at that, it was a tight fit. Huddled together we would order our favorite toasted tea cakes and cups of tea. I just loved it and it was something we did regularly. This was the only "eating out" we did back then and it was wonderful. I can still remember the lovely smell of toasted tea cake and the hiss of the steam from the kettle and tea urn. So small and cozy for sure! When I last visited Bolton I went to the Market Hall to find it had been modernized and initially I was a little put-off, but then really liked what had been done. They had preserved the spirit of the old market and it was a great space, I hope it still is.

The Outdoor Market was in another location near the bus station. It sold meat, poultry, and fish, from many ancient stalls under a roof. Adjoining this permanent part of the market was ground where market traders came twice a week for Market Day. The stalls were closely packed, endlessly fascinating, and had a huge variety of goods for sale, and super salesmen holding forth stridently selling crockery, pans. You name it, they sold it. Markets are so very English. I wish the tradition had been transported to America and that they had thrived here. However, Colonial settlers had a whole lot more to contend with, survival being paramount, and the market tradition didn't cut it. I enjoy going to markets any time I can as they were a happy part of my childhood.

FOOD RATIONS DURING WORLD WAR II

BOLTON, ENGLAND

Chapter Ten

LANCASHIRE FOOD

B olton had a particular fondness for tripe, especially a hot dish called Tripe and Onions. My mother loved it. It just looked so terrible on the butcher's stalls in the market or at the butcher's shop. Folds and piles of the pitted stomach lining and a sickly white color! I tried it once but that was enough for me. My other two experiences with tripe were when I tried a recipe once. It had ginger in it. I don't know what I did wrong, but it was just inedible and got thrown out after one small taste by my husband who will usually eat anything! The third experience was when we were in Normandy and Tripe is their go-to dish in restaurants it seems, so we tried it, Tripe a la Mode. Same result, appalling. So it's off my list, but remains firmly on the Bolton list! Lancashire Hotpot was another big thing back then. Lamb, potatoes, and sliced onions are all packed into an earthenware pot, seasoned, and cooked for a long time in a low oven. Who can forget the way that top layer of potatoes crisped up? We were blessed to have a mother who could not only conjure up meals from practically nothing, a good talent to have in the war years and after, but she was a really excellent cook and whatever she made (except for tripe!) tasted very good. So we enjoyed stellar hotpots. Another Lancashire favorite then was black puddings, blood, and other unmentionables crafted into big fat shapes sort of like a round sausage. Fish and chips were rampant of course, "Chippies" as the shops were known were thick on the ground and no wonder as the food was delicious. Present-day food inspectors would swoon with horror at no doubt countless violations. The fish, deep-fried in excellent batter, was slapped onto a pile of chips, doused with malt vinegar, salt, and pepper from huge shakers, and all wrapped up in a piece of greaseproof paper, and old newspapers. I remember fish being sixpence, chips two pence, and it all was food for the Gods. We had our very own chippie two streets away and an older couple called Lily and Arthur ran it. Arthur was a very serious-looking man with a shock of gray hair and wore a long light brown overall coat thing to work in. He would wield his large scoops as he did all the frying in cavernous deep fryers with smoking hot fat ready and waiting. He slapped the ordered fish into the batter, then delicately eased it into the fryer and was constantly kept busy between that and the one with endless chips on the go. Lily was clad in an enormous flowered pinny and took the orders and the money. You could have mushy peas too, and rows of bottled pop were on a long shelf along the back of the shop. Pop back then was rarely in our budget and it was a huge treat if we ever got any. Tizer, Lemonade, or Orange Crush were on offer, also Dandelion and Burdock and Vimto. Often, I would be sent for two pennorth (two pence worth) of chips and some free scraps, which were bits of batter that had fallen off in the fryer, and then I was to run home fast so we could share them hot. There was always a line at the door waiting for the Chippie to open. The shop was tiny and a high counter divided the cooking area from the waiting area. It was only about two people wide so always a bit of a crush. There was an ancient battered wooden bench for you to sit on if you had to wait. The Chippie was open lunchtime and evenings, usually till quite late so as to serve the "after the pub " crowd! Things could get interesting then as unsteady drinkers would sway inside in a cloud of beer fumes. Nowadays fish and chip shops serve all sorts of things, curry and chips, pies and pasties of all varieties, and a long list of diverse things. Thankfully they have not only survived but flourished, and I LOVE to have fish and chips when I visit. I remember Busy Lizzie's in Skipton. You can buy takeout, or be seated and served, and add bread and butter and cups of tea to your feast. It was so delicious.

Confectioners shops were and still are great features both in town and in numerous locations amongst the streets. They sold meat pies, meat and potato pies, pasties which were all made on the premises. They also made tea cakes, fresh bread, flour cakes, custard tarts, Eccles cakes, Napoleons, iced buns, cream cakes, and a large selection of other wonderful things. Let me not forget the meringues. My Mother's favorite job ever was when she was hired as a helper at Fulgoni's confectionary shop on Rishton Lane near our house. Mr. and Mrs. Fulgoni were Italian but made all the traditional English stuff. Great characters, and good to my mother, and to me, making me welcome if I had to be with her. Mr. Fulgoni and I formed a bond and years later on my wedding day, his son wheeled him out onto the street in his wheelchair, and on my way to the church in the huge black car, we pulled up and I got out in all my finery to give him a hug and a kiss and he gave me his blessing.

One can never forget the Sweet Shops. Devoted to every kind of sweet ever made, these small shops had rows and rows of shelves, each holding large bottles of various sweets, humbugs, lemon sherbets, pear drops, Uncle Joe's Mint balls, wine gums, midget gems, licorice all sorts, mint imperials, dolly mixtures, cough drops, jelly babies and on and on. The variety was staggering. You bought the sweets by them being weighed out. Four ounces was usual, but they would sell you two ounces and they were weighed out on the old scale with weights and then poured into a small white paper bag. When I went to Bolton Grammar School at age 11, I would often walk the long walk from school to the Town Center through Queen's Park, and just outside it was a sweet shop. I'd spend the two-pence bus fare I had saved on whatever I fancied and chomped away happily as I walked on to the connecting bus stop and took my second bus home. It was worth it. During the war and a good while after, rationing meant you could only get a very small amount of sweets per week and I think that an appetite for them built up in me then. (I'm always looking for the roots of my yo-yo ride with my weight all my life!) I certainly built up a desire for sweets when they were so scarce and overindulged whenever I could when rationing was over. Sweet shops are still magical to me when I visit them, the selection is staggering and wonderful but too tempting!

Bolton was blessed to have a very large ice cream shop in the center of town called Tognarellis, known as Togs. It was located over Burton's Men's Wear Store and was on the second level. After climbing the stairs, you entered this large cavernous room with high ceilings and long windows down the length of it facing onto the street. The long counter was on the other side and many tables and chairs were set out next to the windows and in every other available space. It was THE place to go when I was young, especially on Sunday afternoons. It gave us a place to be, to gather with young people from all the surrounding districts of Bolton. You could really have a good time there without spending a fortune. The ice cream was fabulous and they had a squirt of something red to put on top of the ice cream that was divine. The ice cream was served in little glass dishes or big ones if you had more money! Every kind of soft drink was available including sarsaparilla, dandelion and burdock, Tizer, Lemonade, Orange Crush, and the wonderful Vimto. Ice cream was slow to appear but was eventually available after the war, and the small trucks appeared that rumbled slowly up and down the streets announcing their presence with tinkling music. Before that, however, one day just after the war was over, I remember a boy running by our door, clutching a white pudding basin. Then another arrived close behind and I asked what was going on. Gasping and anxious to start galloping again he announced that the shop on Rishton Lane had ice cream, Ice cream? Never heard of it, but it looked like it was obviously a good thing. So my mother and I grabbed a bowl and joined the throng hurrying up to get in the queue and then eat this wonderful stuff. They gave one dollop from a scoop into the motley assortment of bowls, basins, and large cups that people had turned up with. I've never forgotten that day and wonder how the word spread so fast!

There was a similar reaction when bananas arrived after the war was over and men didn't have to die in the merchant ships bringing them to us. This totally strange-looking apparition was turned over and over with curiosity and eventually opened. I have loved them ever since.

I should mention the ever-present pork pies that were sold in butcher's shops or on the market. They were made of jellied seasoned pork filling, and a harder cold water pastry and sometimes there would be a boiled egg in the middle. The pastry was fluted in a traditional way and they were served cold. They came in various sizes from small individual ones that appeared at most functions on the refreshment table, to larger ones you could buy just one slice from. They also appeared on refreshment counters. My brother loved jokes and one day came up with this: "There's a big party going on at the railway station cafe, one of the pork pies is turning 21!"

I mustn't forget the ever-present "tater 'ash", potato hash in posh talk. I still make that occasionally; it's a great way to make a little meat go a long way. I'm sure there's a lot more Lancashire food that I've forgotten. During the war, food was so scarce and everyone made do. It wasn't all that great on a daily basis, but as things eventually developed and began to provide more choice and the chance to restart life was taken, it all improved. With more to cook and more to eat, the old dishes continued with better ingredients. I still love so many of the foods and dishes from my childhood, but I'll end by singing the praises of my favorite thing of all. The Olde Pasty Shoppe in Bolton town center was across from the Olde Man and Scythe, and this old low ceilinged and beamed premises began in the Middle Ages and still does a roaring trade. The line is always long, the aroma totally tantalizing and those pasties can't be beaten in my book! They are served quickly and efficiently by a bevy of women in flowered overalls who swoop them into the paper bag, swing it round to twist the ends and you are out of there pronto. They sell cakes and other confectionery, also meat pies, meat and potato pies, but the top seller for centuries is the pasty, and long may it continue. I can't wait for my next visit.

I should add that these are my memories of food back when I lived there and that's a long time ago. England has moved on and Bolton has too, it's more international and cosmopolitan in the food that is available and eaten now. In fact, the choice is amazing. I am always puzzled that some people will still say British food isn't good. They haven't been in a long time is all I can say because it's amazingly diverse and wonderful nowadays.

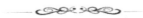

SYLVIA'S ENGLISH TRIFLE
A Special treat at Christmas and Easter

1 pound cake from the store
1 can mandarin oranges
1 can sliced peaches, Cut them into small pieces
1 small can pineapple tidbits
1 pack frozen strawberries, thaw beforehand
2 large boxes of strawberry jell-o
2 Boxes of Vanilla Cook and Serve pudding mix

Cut the pound cake in cubes and put in base of a large serving bowl. Drain the cans of fruit and the thawed strawberries, save the juice. Add the fruit to the bowl. Stir very gently to mix, don't mush up the cake too much. Make the jell-o, using the fruit juices as part of the cold liquid added. Pour the jell-o over the cake and fruit. Chill till set.

When the jell-o is set, make the Vanilla pudding mix as the directions indicate, then pour onto the jell-o and fruit. Return this to the refrigerator and let that set. Just before serving, top with whipped cream and decoration to your liking, cherries, strawberries, sprinkles, or whatever you like. Enjoy!

Sylvia's Recipe for English Fruit Scones

8 oz of Self Raising Flour, or All-Purpose flour
2 oz butter or margarine
1 oz sugar (or more to taste)
2 oz sultanas or raisins
Pinch of salt
6 dessert spoonsfuls of milk

Mix flour, sugar, and butter in food processor. Transfer to a bowl. Add the fruit, then add the milk till it bonds. Use less milk rather than more. Knead a little. Pat dough down to one inch thick. Use cutter to cut out scones. This recipe makes 6 or 7. Brush with a little milk. Place on lightly greased tray. Bake 10-15 minutes at 400 degrees. Keep your eye on them for the last five minutes.

BOLTON'S COAT OF ARMS

Chapter Eleven

ENTERTAINMENT

We might have been in the "North of England," usually shortened to "the North," but Bolton amply provided us with entertainment. My first experience when about six years old was going to the nearby Ritz Cinema on a Saturday afternoon. Known as the Flea Pit, this rather decrepit old cinema would fill up with children of all ages from all directions. The din was deafening, the movies riveting! Tom Mix, Flash Gordon, The Lone Ranger, The Three Stooges, Laurel, and Hardy all had us entranced and kept the noise level at a fever pitch. I just could not handle a terrible serial called "The Clutching Hand." The disembodied hand would appear down chimneys and from unexpected places accompanied by tense, scary music and screams of terror from us. The hand would scuttle about doing terrible things, including choking people, and it gave me nightmares even though I would try to keep my eyes shut. In addition to the relentless din from the audience participation, children threw things, fights would break out, relatively ineffective ushers would try to quell the mayhem. Once it was over, we would eventually all emerge in a happy daze. You can tell that none of us had helicopter parents; we were sent off with sixpence to all this mayhem and good riddance to us for the afternoon!

As I grew older, I graduated to the three cinemas in the Town Center. The Queens, the Capital, and the jewel in our crown, the Odeon. This fantastic place was beautiful, palatial, very art deco, and had an organ that rose from the depths in the interval between the B movie and the top of the bill movie. The lights would come up as the organ played, and ushers in cute outfits with tiny pillbox hats, short skirts, and a large tray kept up by a huge strap around their necks would appear. The tray had little tubs of ice cream that you ate with a miniature wooden spoon and other goodies. The girls stood at the bottom of the aisles, and you went down to buy, standing in a queue, of course, at which we were all very practiced. The movies at the Odeon were a cut above Tom Mix and The Clutching Hand. You got a second B movie, the Newsreel, then the Main feature. The back row was usually inhabited by courting couples wrapped around each other. Norman and I had our turn there quite a few times. It was quite an event and experience to go to the Odeon. The other cinemas were less luxurious and elaborate, but I remember often going to The Capital to see dazzling Hollywood musicals in all their vibrant color spectacle and glitz. It was like looking at another world so far removed from Lancashire life. After the Capital, if I was lucky and had threepence, I could go into Sabrinis, also on Churchgate, and have ice cream before the penny ride home on the bus.

Also on Churchgate were two live theaters, the Theatre Royal and the Grand. How blessed we were to have these live productions in the town. One of my first memories is going to a Variety Show at the Grand with my father. One of the acts was a lion tamer. I was a neophyte theater goer, but even I could sense things weren't going so well. The lion was recalcitrant, looked miserable and surly, and the lion tamer in the cage with it looked increasingly more nervous and apprehensive. Things deteriorated rapidly when the lion had had enough and pounced on the man, pinning him down, jaws clamped on his body. Horror and chaos ensued, one person threw up, and men emerged on stage with sticks to try and pry the lion off. People began screaming and leaving the theater, and total uproar reigned. Later, my father had a great time relating to all who would listen about how we were witnesses to the big event. "Eeeh," 'is "ed was in its mouth." The incident was Headline News in the paper. The Lion Tamer ended up in the Royal Infirmary. I never heard what happened to the lion, but I'm sure it wasn't something good, poor creature. Usually, however, the Variety Shows at the Grand were excellent with comedians, jugglers, skits, acrobats, singers, banter, and lots of audience participation, all well worth a visit.

The Theatre Royal next door was a good bit more refined. I saw Mona Inglesby's ballet there, and I will never forget that my mother found money for me to go every single night. She did the same when the International Ballet came with Alicia Markova and Anton Dolin. There were different ballets every night, and they were just so beautiful and inspiring. I waited at the stage door to see Markova and Dolin and got their autographs, oh joy! I was besotted with ballet then, even more so after that experience. I read all I could, dreamed of being a ballerina, (no chance of that, of course, remember those big limbs!) I even made a pair of ballet shoes out of scraps of satin and ribbons, and this began a habit of going into the "front room" at home, turning the BBC to its classical music programs, and I would dance and dance. What a gift that all was. I'll never know how my mother ever found the money, but she did. I was so grateful then, and I still am. In addition to the ballet, there were musical productions such as the D'Oyly Carte company performing various Gilbert and Sullivan operettas, Concerts, visiting artists, all such excellent stuff. I marvel now at how available it was back then.

On top of all that, Bolton had a Repertory Theater. Every week the company put on a new play, and I saw them all. One of the actresses was Jean Baird, and when I was 16 I got a job babysitting her son Toby on Saturdays and once went to Scotland with Toby, driven up there by his Uncle, to deliver him to Jean's parents who lived in Ayr. I spent two weeks with these beautiful people. Her mother had broken her arm, so I was an extra pair of hands. But back to the repertory theater. It was amazing that each week they served up a different play, and they were well done too.

Then there was the Victoria Hall, to which came the Halle Orchestra based close by in Manchester, and other visiting musical events. The Bolton Town Chorus sang oratorios at Easter and Christmas with imported professional soloists. The Messiah was performed at Christmas and sometimes repeated at Easter, it was much loved. Numerous amateur choruses existed, and there was a strong tradition of choral singing. There were Church choirs, secular choirs, and it all began with Chorus in schools; this was not an option but a regular feature of the curriculum from elementary school on up, and we would sing the old songs together.

So as I look back now, there was plenty to do, and I am so grateful for experiencing it all. I'm incredibly thankful to my mother, who always came up with the money for me to go. She was amazing that way and seemed to feel she wanted to encourage my interest in all these things and made it possible. Although she had such a meager income, she could squirrel away money and nearly always have it available for something for my brother and me. When she died, my father and I sorted out her things and quickly learned we had better be vigilant. We found pound notes in the most unlikely places; in the seams of an old corset, in the toes of her best shoes neatly stored in the shoe boxes, hidden in tins behind the towels, hidden in baking pans at the back of the kitchen cupboard. Money was also in the toes of socks, nylons, and various ornaments. It was quite a treasure trove, and my father was astounded; he never knew she did this. I think it was her way of controlling something, but I bless her for providing me with all these experiences. She had to put her own dreams and hopes on hold all her life, but she made many dreams of mine come true and encouraged my interest in the arts. It was a Godsend, and I love her for it.

Chapter Twelve

CHILDHOOD OCCUPATIONS

As young children, our main playground was the immediate area, our five or six streets, with occasional forays to slightly further afield. Post- World War II was a bit grim, but we could always "play out" and we did, endlessly. You knew every kid in the immediate area, and our parents were happy to have us out of the house. In the evening, as dusk drew in, the mothers would stand at their doors and shout the name of their child or children over and over, resounding around the streets, and as this chorus of calls increased, we would reluctantly start going home.

What did we get up to? Well, things came in waves. Top and Whip was fun though it all depended on if you had one or you were a spectator. I remember we would chalk patterns on the top so it would look prettier when spinning. You had to practice a lot, wrapping the whip around the wooden top with its metal tip and then mastering the art of giving it that perfect flick that sent it careening off the whip onto the ground where it would spin on its steel tip. At the right season, we would go on conker hunting expeditions to the nearest horse chestnut tree, which was quite a way off. The nuts grew in a prickly green casing, and once they fell, you stripped the green part off and you you were left with a hard, shiny, brown, and good-sized nut. The conker. We seasoned them to try and make them harder, sometimes with vinegar or whatever else we could come up with. Then with an adult's help, we would suspend them on a string, and we were off, let the conker wars begin! You held your conker still, suspended on its string, and your competitor would launch his conker at yours, hoping to break it. You took turns. Inevitably someone would have a prize conker that soon emerged, larger and harder than anyone else's, and it would end up the Champion! When that fad faded, skipping ropes would come into vogue. We loved to do it endlessly, individually or using a long rope that two would turn while others took turns jumping into it and performing what skills they had. We'd jump in one after another, keeping things going, till someone got caught up in the rope. We knew so many rhymes to chant as we did this, and I am sorry now that I didn't write them down. We would skip rope individually, counting as we went, doing double unders, and it all kept us busy. Suddenly, as if we heard through the ether, ropes would be out, and we were all into marbles. Every kid had a bag, and there was some game the boys seemed to have invented and controlled that ended up with one person getting more and more marbles. The rules were incredibly flexible, and it was mostly who could con who that they had lost. You hated to "lose your marbles" and see them carried off in triumph in someone else's drawstring bag. Marbles tended to cause a lot of quarreling and tears, but they had their day.

If someone had a piece of chalk, hopscotch became the game of the moment. Games would keep us busy until tea time. We would love it in winter if the pavement became iced over, and one year we worked tirelessly to smooth out a very long slide. We took turns, taking a long run at it, then launching on to it, and away you would go to the end, usually upright, but occasionally not. It was a truly exceptional slide that year, but of course, when we were all called in for tea, the slide remained, a danger zone for unsuspecting pedestrians right outside the corner shop. We came in for many muttered curses.

There were many brick walls at the end of streets, and we would do handstands up against them. It never seemed to bother us that our knickers were showing! The more flexible would do "the crab." I managed it a few times, but my back was never all that flexible. Then would come the French cricket time, but this depended on someone having a bat and someone else having a ball! Most of us were fielders, but the wide wooden bat sent the tennis ball flying, and we were all kept busy. Playing on cobbled streets was quite an accomplishment, and thankfully we all made it in one piece! If someone had a larger ball, we would play dodge ball or pig in the middle, the pig jumping up like crazy to try and intercept it. Suddenly the "in thing" to do would be to play balls against the brick end of the row. Overs, unders, how long could you keep it up, sort of like juggling against the wall. Somehow, we would all get hold of at least two balls, and sometimes people played with three going. The poor souls who lived in the end houses must have grown weary with the endless pounding of balls against the house wall. We tried to move on to different walls and not drive any single neighbor mad for too long.

On some occasions, we would play Simon Says. The whole cobbled street would be full of kids, all playing and peacefully sitting out if they messed up and moved and the leader told them they were out. We were well trained to be rule followers in those days, and there was no whining; we would peacefully go and sit on the edge of the pavement. "London Bridge is Falling Down" had its day, also Ring around the Rosy. The Ring around the Rosy game had been around since plague times.

In addition to all the cyclical games, I was always coming up with imagination games. I remember a long-running Blue Fairy one. Everyone had a part, and events in Blue Fairyland would happen, all directed by bossy me, though no one seemed to mind. Another long-running game I came up with was The Lorrimers; this was a la Little Women, about a family in Victorian days and went on for weeks. We never could wait to get outside and see what the Lorrimers would get up to, as directed by "Moi." As an adult, I visited Bolton and reconnected with one of my old playmates. Barbara had married and still lived next door to her parents on the old street, as was the old way. She was glad to see me, and the first thing she said was, "Oh, I still remember the Blue Fairy Game!"

One day the word spread that the chimney at an abandoned cotton mill nearby was to be demolished and brought down. Crowds gathered, and we breathlessly watched all the preparations, and the action as police and others kept us all at bay. Then BOOM, down it came in that slow-motion implosion collapse that is so fascinating. A cloud of centuries-old dust followed the collapse, and that got us all out of our spell and into fits of coughing and scurrying to move even further back. It was a great event for us and the source of much talk for a while.

Another activity we were all very invested in was the annual Guy Fawkes Night. After a hiatus during the war, every November 5th, bonfires were (and still are) set all over England to commemorate the failure of the plot hatched by the said Guy Fawkes to blow up the Houses of Parliament. Of course, we needed wood, so for a couple of months, we were on endless hunts to find some. There wasn't a tree in the immediate vicinity, so off we would go, hoping to find something to burn on our bonfire when the day came. Anything found would be dragged back and stored on the roofs of the outside privies in the back streets. I had a friend called Donald Yates at the top of the next street. He was three or four years older than me, but we were often a team. We had been on a firewood search after school with no luck at all. Despondently, we were winding our way home for our tea, and as we turned into the back street, three or four houses down, we were transfixed to see a wooden door leaning against the outside wall, apparently abandoned. Donald and I exchanged excited and triumphant glances and promptly carried it down to my house. Somehow, we got it onto the privy roof and added it to our woodpile. We were SO happy, but that all faded very soon! Ten minutes later, I was inside eating my tea(yes, we ate our tea in the North, but that's another story) when an uproar seemed to be going on in the back street. An irate apoplectic man was cursing and blinding out there, and we all went through the tiny backyard and gingerly opened the yard gate to see what was going on. My father was appalled as the gist of the tirade sunk home. The man had taken his door off its hinges to paint it, had gone in because his tea was ready, only to emerge and find the door gone. A short search had revealed it up there on our woodpile. My Father's eyes turned on me, never a good thing, and I beat a hasty retreat, leaving the adults to sort it all out. The door was returned, the uproar died down, and Donald and I kept low profiles for a good long while. Guy Fawkes night would arrive, and a huge bonfire was lit with the fruits of our labors. Traditional things to eat on that night were treacle toffee, a gingery cake called Parkin, and 'tater pies. We kids put potatoes into the fire, and once these blackened objects were looking like grenades, they were retrieved and eaten. Well, I should say we tried to eat them as they were terrible! Thick black charcoal-covered raw potato. They promised much, were long-awaited, but delivered little! Always hungry, we ate them anyway! The Guy was a sort of scarecrow-like effigy of Guy Fawkes dressed in the odd clothes anyone had been able to spare. We would sit this pitiful object on a stool on the pavement with a sign saying Penny for the Guy, hoping to collect something to use to buy fireworks. All families purchased a few and pooled them. Between us all, we had quite a show with Roman Candles, Silver Starbursts, Catherine Wheels, Sparklers, and a few rockets. There were some horrible things called squib crackers or bangers, and you could count on the boys to be chucking them into the middle of things causing cursing and mayhem on all sides. Later in my life, I became a Catholic and ruefully remembered my years of watching a Catholic being burnt in effigy to the cheers and excitement of the Church of England crowd, me included. The Guy's burning was the crowning moment of the event, celebrating that centuries ago, the plot was foiled, the conspirators arrested and put to death. Bonfire night still lives on.

An activity that came into vogue regularly was to ride the bus to the train station if we had the penny for the fare. If we didn't, we walked, even though it was quite a long way, but that was never a problem in those days. We would take a little notebook and pencil, put ourselves in the middle of the footbridge over the railway lines, and patiently wait for the trains to come by. Local trains had ordinary old engines, but the city to city trains were special and pulled at great speed by particular engines, called Namers. They each had a proud and individual name on the side of the engine. The cream of the crop was The Flying Scotsman, flying by from Edinburgh on its way to London. London was the El Dorado of my world! There would be lots of steam, noise, and clamor as it streaked by, and we would be beside ourselves, capering about in excitement on the narrow, rickety footbridge. Then you wrote that Namer into your notebooks as part of the list of what you saw that day and what time. There was something exciting and promising about seeing those splendid engines and the trains roaring along in clouds of steam to parts far beyond our usual boundaries. A resolve seemed to have always been in my heart, and grew all the time, that I would be on one of those Namers one day and go to London. Those powerful engines breathed the smoke and steam of parts unknown and let you know there was a beyond.

People often say now, oh, it was safe to let children play out back then. Sadly that wasn't true; we had our share of penis flashers, even a man who was at the dell under the bridge with a thorn in his you know what, trying to entice some naive child to come over and assist in the removal. Some men would try to touch you in the movies given half a chance, and once as a small child, I was riding in a bus sitting on my Grandmother's knee, yet I was groped by the man sitting next to us. So no, I don't think it was safer, and at some point, in our childhood, a young girl from our district called Sheila Fox disappeared. No one has ever forgotten that, and we had talks from the police, in school, and from our parents, who presumably had wised up a little after that tragic event. Sadly, Sheila was never found and never lived a long life.

One of my main occupations was to read. We were blessed with the libraries. The Bolton Central Library in the Town Center was one of the earliest public libraries established after the Public Libraries

Act of 1850. It opened in 1853. The branches were well stocked, and I am so grateful for our Great Lever Branch. When I was three years old, my mother took me there, and I got a card. Thus began my saga of many, many trips to that building. I started to read at four years old and was obsessed with books and love them to this day. All the Enid Blytons, Biggles, Swallows and Amazons, and so much more were devoured. Unfortunately, the library janitor was a creepy man who often appeared and hovered about if you were alone in the Children's Section; thank God for the instincts that made me leave whenever he appeared.

Looking back, we were not short of things to do, outside and in. I didn't even mention the knitting and sewing lessons from my mother. I learned to knit, but a potholder was pretty much it, while she quickly produced elaborate and complicated Irish Fisherman Sweaters. I learned embroidery stitches at home and school and would make tray cloths (though we never used a tray), and the odd sampler with the different stitches set out in rows. We also did something with a cotton reel, four nails in the top of it; then you wound wool, lifting it over each pin to make a long snake appear from the bottom of the reel. Another of my mother's favorites was making little dolls from clothes pegs, the old kind, with a round top and long body, divided at the bottom. Then there was Cat's Cradle with string. I could play that for hours and also with the fortune-telling thing you made with folded paper and then said a rhyme till it stopped. You then undid the piece in the middle and read the fortune. These all kept us busy on rainy nights. Looking back, I can truly say that the philosophy seemed to be that idle hands were not a good thing, but I think I benefitted! I didn't turn out to be very crafty until now in my old age when I love to knit again. The entire American continent is in danger of being covered with the knitted blankets that I keep turning out!

The Olde Man & Scythe

Oldest Building in Bolton

Chapter Thirteen

RANDOM REFLECTIONS

Bolton grew because it provided so much work. The cotton mills were in full force in my childhood. I remember we had gone on a walk and reached a high point from which you could see most of the town spread out below, a forest of cotton mills and factory chimneys. Around 240 mills once operated in Bolton. The view was impressive, though not beautiful, and the chimneys were all belching out smoke. There were still active coal mines in the area then, so the "working class" (that was all of us in the streets,) grew and grew. Endless rows of houses were built around the town center with back streets in the rear. As I said in an earlier chapter, we began in Cecilia Street but eventually moved up a notch to Richelieu Street, pronounced Richy Loo, (the Cardinal must have turned over in his grave at this mangling of his name!). I often wonder how that name came to the town planner involved. My grandmother lived in Melbourne Street; she had about a yard wide strip in front of her house, so teeny tiny, and it contained a struggling privet hedge. You could hardly call it a garden, but it was a step up from nothing at all. All the smoke and soot in the area made it a harsh environment for all living things, and the old joke was "Even the pigeons have coughs!" After Melbourne Street, you came to Parkfield Road, and then you were really up in the world. The houses were just slightly larger all around. Above them, you reached the Avenues, really beyond our reach, semi-detached houses, with a front and a rear garden and indoor plumbing.

So I remember in the cold dark mornings of the 1940s hearing the "knocker up" at work. This man was the poor soul whose job it was to get up before dawn and trudge along the streets with a long pole and knock on the upstairs windows of his clients to get them awake. Then the noise of feet walking by began. They streamed by our house to the cotton mills nearby, many of them wearing clogs that were still in use then. Clogs were huge sabot-like things, sturdy, strong, with strips of iron lining the soles. Women wore shawls over their heads, coats, and overalls, and off they would go to work well before the sun was up. My mother made the best of a bad job and swore that clogs were good for you and strengthened the ankles! I only ever had one pair; the theory was they lasted forever. I felt like I had weights on my feet, like The Prisoner of Zenda! I did finally outgrow them and vowed never again.

I know the phrase "knocker up" caused great amusement when I innocently used it in my later years in America. It has a totally different meaning to Americans, as we all know! You would say, "I'll knock you up" if you were planning an outing together and going to come by and make sure they were ready. Or to be called in the morning was to be "knocked up." Also, playing tennis, you had a preliminary knock-up before you began to play, so if you came out with this phrase, you caused consternation in Americans followed by shocked hilarity! I soon learned to drop it from my vocabulary!

From twelve years old, my parents worked in the cotton mills, which were dangerous places to be in as a child with all that machinery clattering away. The high humidity maintained in the factory for the sake of the cotton didn't help my father's wonky respiratory system. His father had died of tuberculosis when my Dad was a young child, and he developed problems himself. It led to him taking up swimming, which proved to be a wonderful thing for him all his life. There were Municipal Swimming Baths throughout the town as many houses didn't have bathrooms. My father became a beautiful and accomplished swimmer. He played water polo and was also a very good diver as a young man. A few months after he married my mother, he dived into the swimming pool, hit the bottom, and had a fractured skull. Medical care was scanty and next to nothing, and he was carried on a board to a nearby house. I'm not sure what else happened, but he didn't go to the hospital. I think a doctor eventually saw him, but as soon as possible, he was carried by his mates on a board to his own home and left to hope for recovery. He then had to let nature take its course and hope healing would come. He did survive, but my mother said that from that time on, he was a changed personality, prone to anger and irritability. But I digress! Back to the cotton mill. My mother loved working in the mill. She said she was good at it, which made her happy, and she also enjoyed the camaraderie, shared cups of tea, and the whole thing. They might have been "dark satanic mills," but she made the best of it. She worked as a piecer and then a spinner controlling these giant, noisy machines. I remember going to the mill to deliver a message to her once and stepping into this huge cavernous room filled with machinery, shuttling back and forth in a cacophony of continuous noise. There were bits of cotton lint floating in the air, huge belts rolling by overhead, and the steamy humid atmosphere was suitable for the cotton, but not the people. At other times in her life, my mother did house cleaning jobs in one of the avenues. Her favorite job was to work at Mr. and Mrs. Fulgoni's Bakery and

Confectionery Shop as previously mentioned. She was an excellent cook and loved using her skills on cakes, pies, sweet and savory things, and her days passed happily. Mr. Giovanni Fulgoni reminded her of her father. Mr. Fulgoni was large, quiet most of the time unless he got into a dispute and upset, then his Italian heritage emerged in all its flamboyant glory!

My father had to leave the cotton mill due to his health problems. The doctor advised him to find a job in the open air, which always seemed like a dubious recommendation to me considering the sparrows and pigeons hacking and coughing all over the place. I don't think I would have known what to do in his circumstances, no work, no prospect of any, very little education, no money, no savings, but a family to provide for. Undeterred, he purloined my mother's step ladder and bucket, invested in a good chamois leather and a supply of neat rags, and began his life as a window cleaner. Off he marched, round to my grandmother's house in Melbourne Street and cleaned her windows for ninepence. His first paying customer! He built a "Window Cleaning Round" from there, and in all weathers, he set off with his ladder and bucket. In time he had a bicycle and balanced it all as he rode from street to street. I still have his ledger accounts book with the meticulous handwritten records of his business. The first entry is August 25th, 1945, and in that week, his entries were Window Cleaning 19 shillings 1 penny, Gardening and odd jobs earned one pound and eleven shillings. So he had earned Two pounds, ten shillings, and one penny total, about $3.50. The ledger is well kept, each week has its total, and on the right-hand side of the page were his expenses. New leathers were seven shillings and sixpence, a new ladder at one point, three pounds seventeen shillings and sixpence. His insurance was nine shillings for 12 weeks, and the odd gardening or painting job was included in the mix. His yearly income for 1945-1946 was one hundred and twenty pounds, two shillings and ten pence- about $300. His expenses were about $30. Our livelihood depended on the weather and such odd jobs that he could add-in. His last entry for 1969-1970 was a total earned for the year of five hundred and two pounds, thirteen shillings and ninepence, not even $1,000. It was a different world. He worked hard in all weathers; he was never "on the dole," he lived on what he earned and worked for.

I began to work during the school holidays when I was old enough. My first venture was as a waitress in the Bus Station Cafe in town for a shockingly short time! Let's just say my tolerance for cheeky bus drivers and conductors was very low! My demise came when they were all driving me crazy with innuendo, weak jokes, etc., and I appeared with a plate of egg and bacon ordered by one particularly obnoxious Romeo. He proceeded to tell me that that wasn't what he had asked for, and I totally lost it, banged the plate down in front of him, and said,

"THAT'S what you're getting." The boss and I came to a mutual decision that it wasn't the job for me.

I quickly got a job at Townleys Hospital in the section known as The Annex. It was where the elderly went to die. I was a charwoman enveloped in an overall and big apron, kitted out with a broom, an enormous bucket, a scrubbing brush about two feet long, and a huge mop. There were long, long corridors, and I would start at one end on my knees and scrub my way to the other end in what seemed like an endless journey over the linoleum. One day a pair of sensibly clad feet appeared in front of me. I raised my eyes to find MATRON standing there, immaculate in her navy blue uniform and a starched white head covering they probably wore in the Crimean War. Now I don't know how it is in hospitals today, but MATRON was a formidable authority figure back then. You spoke when spoken to, and your response was, "Yes, Matron." I wondered what on earth I had done to merit such focus of attention. She actually spoke to me, and I stumbled to my feet, two-foot scrubbing brush in hand. "Are you the girl from Bolton School?" she asked.   I answered with a subdued "Yes." I was given a scholarship to go there when I was 11 years old. It was the top Grammar School in the area and had a lot of prestige. I was blessed to be there. "Why are you in a cleaning job?" Matron asked. I said that had been the only job offered. "Ridiculous," she said, "Tomorrow, you will be

- 105 -

a nursing aide." And that was that. She swept on up the corridor. Back on my knees and mopping away, my jangling nerves calmed down, and I welcomed this turn of events! So the next day, I reported for duty and was given a nurse's uniform, a different color to the ones worn by those who knew what they were doing, but best of all, I had one of those starched white nurse caps with a pleated fall at the back and I loved the starch white. I also the starched white bib aprons that were issued. So began my new job. There were times when I wondered if mop bucket for bedpan had been a good trade, but under Nurse Edward's maternal eye, I learned how to make hospital beds even with people in them, give baths, and deliver and remove bedpans. On some days, the two of us had three large wards to work through, hurrying to answer buzzers elsewhere, scurrying back to work together to get patients up, make up their beds, see to those who couldn't get up, deal with bedsores, changing bed linens, giving sponge-downs, and so on. I soon saw my first dying person, and then when she had passed on, was taught how to layout and minister to dead bodies. I was 16, it was very heavy stuff, but I felt useful and learned a lot.

Walking home after work, I had to walk by what was then known as the Mental Ward. Outside, a dozen or so patients were equipped with hoes and rakes, standing on the grass, leaning on the tools, and mainly gazing into the distance and completely immobile.

With them was a nurse or orderly, and he was working away on the flower beds. As I went by, he said with a nod at the passive, relaxed group doing nothing, "It makes you wonder who is bloody daft around here, doesn't it!" and he wearily turned back to his hoeing.

The Annex stood separate from the main hospital in an old building that had previously been the area Workhouse. My grandmother lived in fear of ending up in the Workhouse, as did most of the elderly poor. Things had changed, but they didn't believe it. It had been a dreaded place for centuries, and in their minds, it still was. Workhouses were so often Dickensian, stark, and the place of last resort. All of the elderly in the area felt negative about the Annex because of its history. It was still "The Workhouse" in their minds, no matter what new-fangled name it had acquired. When my grandmother grew ill, as her life drew to a close and she knew she was going to go to the hospital, her constant fear was that she would go to the Workhouse. Once there, her repeated question was, "Am I in the Annex?" Once settled though, she got good care and relaxed, for which we were thankful.

There were other part-time jobs along the way, and I look back now and am glad for the experience each one brought me.

Photo of Sylvia's Mother, Ellen Luke

outside the Corner Shop

Chapter Fourteen

BOLTON HOLIDAYS

So let me see what I remember about Bolton Holidays. Other mill towns surrounded Bolton and the custom was that each town, Bury, Wigan, Blackburn, Oldham, Rochdale, etc was designated a certain week when all could go on holiday. This prevented the seaside resorts from being totally overrun by all of us at one time and presumably ensured that some industrial production would continue somewhere at all times. Eventually, it became two weeks. During Bolton Holidays, the shops and markets closed, the corner shop being the only remaining resource if you were unfortunate enough not to have gone away with the rest of the town. The town was mostly empty as there was a mass exodus to the seaside, Blackpool being the favorite back then. Cleveleys, Fleetwood, Southport, and Bispham were not far behind. Crowds of people clutching suitcases descended on Trinity Street Station when the day arrived; special trains hauled everyone off, leaving a ghost town behind. Extraordinary when you think of it, but I don't remember hearing about burglaries happening or anything. Let's face it, most of us didn't have a lot to steal. As a small child, I woke up on THE day after days of excitement leading up to the Exodus, feeling nauseous, having worked myself up into what my mother called a state of nerves. I finally threw up and felt a lot better but remained overexcited. We stood in the queues for the bus to the station, finally got there, and jostled shoulder to shoulder with everyone else down to the platform. It was crowded with rather grim-looking holidaymakers, already frazzled by the bus queues, carrying cases, queuing for train tickets, and now in the crowds on the platform. I was clutching my much beloved stuffed rabbit. I must have been three or four, but I can still remember the occasion very well. A buzz ensued as we heard the train approaching in all the glory of the steam trains, grinding noise, clouds of steam, and in the sudden activity all around, I stepped forward to try and see this giant engine properly, when oops, my rabbit flew out of my hands and onto the track. I was horrified and wailed inconsolably. Stuffed rabbits were hard to come by, and I loved mine. A kindly uniformed guard came to the rescue, and once the train had halted, he got a broom, fished my rabbit out, and returned it to me. Clutching it, hiccupping, and sniffing, I was swept up into the third-class carriage and squashed up like everyone else. Doors eventually were banged shut, like a barrage of shots; the whistle blew, and the guard majestically waved his large green flag, then hauled himself up into the last carriage. Shuddering, straining, belching smoke and steam, off we went. We were soon clackety clacking in that distinctive rhythm that was quite hypnotic, and we were finally on our way. The train was packed and since all were going to the same place it made no stops. Everyone settled down for the trip. Out would come sandwiches, the thermos of tea, and bottles of ale, and the time passed. Soon you could hear the shout passed down the train by heads sticking out of the windows. "There it is! There it is!" the famous Blackpool Tower, visible for miles and such a Northern landmark. Heads craned through the windows, everyone got a turn, and yes, there it was, a smaller version of the Eiffel Tower, a symbol of the SEASIDE indeed. Once we pulled into the station, everyone disembarked. In a much more relaxed mood, the crowd scattered to the various boarding houses that provided Bed and Breakfast and tea if you were lucky. These establishments were run by martinets, whose word was law and seemed to think this was still the Edwardian times, and they were running some kind of penitentiary. Some were more benevolent rulers than others, thank goodness. Blackpool had the Tower, the Tower Circus, The Tower Ballroom (later to feature in my life as the place where I met my future husband when I was 19). There were amusement parks, rides, the famous Big Dipper, visible for miles. The beautiful promenade was known to all as The Prom. It had strategically placed shelters that you could cower and take refuge in if the weather was cold, windy, and rainy, always a good possibility in an English summer. It also had wondrous trams attached by a flexible pole to the electric line above, and these went up and down the coast. I loved them. They went all the way to Bispham and Fleetwood. On the Sands were herds of little donkeys, bells tinkling as they were trotted down onto the sands every morning and back again in the evening. Donkey rides were a big thing. I had one ride per holiday, which was considered enough on our budget. There were piles of deck chairs for hire along the beach and the sea wall. The tide went far out, leaving a huge expanse of beach and lots of pools, rocks, and shells. Every child seemed to have a bucket and spade, and making sandcastles was very popular. They sold windmills that you could stick into the top of your castle, and round it would go like a dervish. There was nearly always a sharp wind from the Irish Sea. The sea was very, very cold, pretty much all the time, so one paddled rather than jumping in and swimming. Bathing suits weren't too common back then, but just in case there were hardier souls, there were rows of cabins for changing under the sea wall. The waves were usually strong. I do love to be near the sea. Wherever you are in England, you are rarely more than 50 miles away from the coast, and the sea swept its way into my heart early in my life and has never left. Once married, we lived for five years in Jamaica and 17 years in St Croix in the Virgin Islands. It was so wonderful to be able to go to the Caribbean Sea so easily after work, and certainly at weekends. There's something so primal and universal about the sea, its ebb and flow, and endless action. It was here before us and will be here after us. I cherish any time I can get to the ocean. I am so happy just to sit near it, any season of the year. It answers some longing in my soul. However, I digress, back to Blackpool. We mostly stayed in Fleetwood, which was much quieter and less expensive. The large fishing fleet sailed out each day, returning to port late afternoons, and I loved to see them. There were huge rock formations in Fleetwood leading down to the shore. They were wonderful for climbing and jumping and generally exploring all over them. On the streets leading down from your boarding house to the sea, you would pass endless Fish and Chip Shops and Shellfish stalls selling winkles and cockles that were eaten with a pin or a stick. There were lots of tearooms and cafes selling "butties" (sandwiches), cakes, and cups of tea. The shops that sold buckets and spades, windmills, and other beach paraphernalia always had several racks on the street full of postcards. There were views of the town you were in, the fishing fleet, the trams, the countryside around, and so on, but mostly they were salacious saucy postcards with vulgar humor showing lots of backsides and bosoms, etc. and filled with sly innuendo. And some not so sly! Some were quite shocking. Everyone seemed to love perusing these bawdy cards and trying to look as if they weren't! Children, including me, had a fascination for them and would try to sneak looks before some adult yelled at them to go away! I wonder if they still have them? You could also buy rock candy everywhere. This was a sweet peppermint confection that came in sticks of various lengths and colors and imprinted in the center would be the name of the town. Rock was wonderful! You could suck it into long points or crunch it if you were careful with your terrible English teeth! It mostly came in pink with a white inside, but other colors too. Taking a stick of rock home for someone still back in the empty ghost town was the thing to do. Wonderful stuff.

The piers in English seaside towns are impressive, long and wide with a theater partway down, a place for dances, an orchestra, or band concerts, and so much to see as you strolled up and down. You had to watch out for the wind though! Seagulls were year-round residents, of course. I remember that there were some simply huge ones in England. They had aggressive-looking beaks and a rather militant manner. They'd launch bombing raids to swoop down and snatch a sandwich right out of an unsuspecting hand! There were smaller gulls and seabirds, but the gangster big boys made quite an impression. They're still at it. Many years later, a friend and I ate a pasty in Truro, sitting on the sea wall, and were appalled to see one of these huge birds swoop down and snatch a large pasty right out of the hand of a man sitting there peacefully with it halfway to his mouth! We beat a hasty retreat!

So, to strains of George Formby singing "Oh, I do like to be beside the seaside", I reluctantly leave my memories of Bolton Holidays. It was often cold and rainy, and those landladies often wouldn't let you be back inside till tea time, even if it was raining. But, you were away, somewhere different, breathing in the bracing sea air of course, and seeing new sights, truly a welcome break from routine!

RICHELIEU STREET IN 1961,

IT HAD COME UP IN THE WORLD.

Chapter Fifteen

CARTS AND HORSES

L ife was enlivened by regular visits from the milkman early every morning. Empty glass bottles were washed and put out on the front steps with a paper stuck in the top to say how many pints were needed that day. The milk cart was a small electric thing with the milkman in a white coat (well, it started out white!) and a jaunty hat. He would jump off at each stop to run over to the doorstep, collect the empties and leave the new full bottles. Milk came in glass bottles, with a foil cap on them, and the tale is often told of how the birds in one part of England figured out that if they pecked away at that silver foil top, they could then happily drink the cream that had risen to the top of the bottle. It took about two weeks for that knowledge and discovery to spread from bird to bird over the whole country. Hence, the housewives of the British Isles all stepped outside one morning to find demolished caps and the top of the milk gone, and that was how it was from then on unless you tried to foil them (no pun intended!) by being right there when the milkman dropped them off. Not a bird in sight, mind you. They were sensibly discreet.

All of this talk of how milk was delivered reminds me of how it came to me when we lived in Mandeville, Jamaica from 1959 to 1964. We would hear a knock on our back kitchen door. We would open it to find Henry standing there. He was a little wizened gentleman dressed fetchingly in some sort of sack over ragged trousers and no shoes. He held in his hand a rope, and at the other end of this was his cow. "How much milk today Madam?" he would ask, and we would hand over a container, a bowl, or a pan, and he would then proceed to milk the cow into it, and with a flourish, he would hand the container back to us now full of warm milk. I couldn't help thinking it was probably full of tuberculosis germs or whatever as well, but this was my milk delivery, and it was that or Pet Evaporated Milk all the time! We would pay Henry, and off he would go over the back garden to the next house, the patient cow plodding behind him! Of course, we boiled the milk before using it, but I have never forgotten our milk deliveries!

Back in Bolton, the Coal Delivery man was another matter. The cart was large and black with soot and looked like it had seen previous use collecting the dead during the Black Plague. It creaked along, pulled by a large dray horse, very gentle and patient but totally dispirited. The bags of coal were stacked on the back and dropped off as ordered by the housewife, who would appear at her door yelling out how many sacks she needed. It was never very many as budgets were pretty strict. The coalman was usually in indescribably filthy clothes that looked so stiff with coal dust and dirt that they looked as if they spent the night on a chair by his bed, and that every morning he would sit up, whistle, and they would get up and walk over to him all by themselves. The coalman would hop off the front of the cart, go round and hump a heavy sack of coal on his back and drop it off at the backyard gate. As kids, we would hopefully follow the coal cart, carrying any receptacle we could find, and pick up any stray pieces that dropped. There were never very many, and there was hot competition for what there was. The universally used coal fires caused buildings to be coated with black soot and dirt, and for years I believed that our fancy Town Center buildings were made of black stone. It was a total revelation when the buildings were cleaned and emerged transformed many years later! That didn't happen until there were few to no coal fires anymore, and the cotton mills were no longer emitting out dark smoke from their chimneys. My mother dried as much of the washing as she could indoors, for as she said, "Put them outside, and it either rains or they end up spotted with black dirt." She had a rack suspended from the kitchen ceiling and pulled the clothes up and down on a rope. She also had a couple of "maidens", wooden contraptions that unfolded to provide bars to hang clothes on. But washing is a topic for another day! I digress.

The other regular visitor was the Rag and Bone man. He had a smaller cart with fatter and quieter wheels. He sat on the front of the cart, guiding his poor horse that looked like it was on its last legs. He would constantly yell, "Rag and Bone, Rag and Bone," at the top of his lungs. Out would come ladies who had something they wanted to get rid of or trade for something. He usually gave donkey stones for whitening front steps or clothes pegs in trade, or nothing at all if it wasn't much of an offering. Our Rag and Bone man wasn't a jolly soul. He was short-tempered and dour, and one day as I sat on the front step with Bruce, my dog friend from next door, Mr. Rag and Bone began to lay into his horse, who for some reason didn't want to move on. I'm afraid I created a scene. Without thinking, I was up on my feet and over there shouting at him in a fury to leave that horse alone. People emerged to see what was happening as I stood yelling at the man to stop. He paused, whip raised in his hand, and looked a bit shocked. Then, glancing at the audience that had gathered, he was a bit disconcerted. He stopped hitting the horse, thank goodness, and I regained my senses and felt rather shocked at myself. Children just did not yell at adults ever.

Occasionally, Gypsies would arrive. Their caravans wouldn't be visible, but they would move from whatever piece of spare ground they had found to park on and fan out through the streets, knocking on doors, offering clothespegs or fortunes. Everyone was very suspicious of the Gypsies, a state of affairs they used to their advantage. People would buy a little something just to have them leave and not be on their bad side, ending up with the evil eye on them or something.

So horses still played quite a part in our lives, poor beasts. It couldn't have been easy for them in the middle of an industrial town.

The War Memorial

Chapter Sixteen

ROUNDUP OF MEMORIES

I remember some things that haven't found a spot in a previous chapter, so I'll give them a place here in a sort of roundup in no particular order. Bolton Wanderers were our much-loved Football Team playing at Burnden Park within walking distance from our house. It was a good walk but very doable. Back then, the players were local lads known to everyone, neighbors of many of us, and supported by all. On Saturdays, when the team was playing at home, beginning mid-morning, a steady stream of men came walking through the streets, all on their way to the match. The crowds made a sort of marching sound passing by our house, like an invading army. They were all in good spirits, and many wore long black and white knitted scarves, and the flat Lancashire caps to keep the chill-out. A few women went, but it seemed to be mainly men. My father had a job as a checker at a turnstile and was very proud of his inside position at The Wanderers. When he retired after over forty years of doing it, he received a lifetime pass to go on the ground. He received this gift from the Club before the big new super stadium replaced Burnden Park. In time football changed, becoming very international with players from all over the world, and very pricey to attend. It was cheap to go and stand back then, and I often went with my grandfather. He had his thermos of tea with his rum in it to ward off the cold. It was such a huge event to be at the match. You could hear the swelling roars of the crowd from our house, and that was impressive. If you were there, it was overwhelmingly loud and got louder as more beer and spirits were drunk. Our eyes were riveted to the field and as part of the crowd, it was like being one of a murmuration of swallows. The huge crowd reacted as one, with roars of excitement and jubilation if we scored, groans and a dull roar if there was little action, or the other team scored. The crowds yelled a lot to the players. "Get stuck in yer maudie lot" "Gerrup yer soft devil, there's nowt wrong with yer" "Nay, don't worry" (this as a player lay prone and lifeless on the pitch), "e'll be up as soon as ref has bin by" Then, of course, lots of "Pass it yer daft bugger" and "By gum, they're bloody useless" "Get rid of it…Get rid of it…" and so on and so on. As you can see, advice flowed freely. One year after the terrible plane crash that killed so many Manchester United players, we ended up in the Cup Final with them at Wembley. The entire country wanted United to win. Who wouldn't? Well, the thousands from Bolton who arrived at Euston Station in London and walked grimly into Wembley Stadium didn't want them to win, no room for sentiment. We won that match, unpopular as we were, and all credit to United for getting so close with so many players missing and gone forever. Thanks to his connections, my father got three tickets for that Cup Final. Quite a feat. One for me, one for Norman, and of course himself. It was fantastic to be there and see the Wanderers win. Quite an experience and a much-envied one. The Cup Final tickets were and still are like gold.

I was sixteen years old before I had a ride in a car. Public transport was excellent, and you could get everywhere without having a car. Cars were a definite big-time status symbol. I was also 16 before I saw a television. The first ones were so small, black and white, and the family of a friend got one for the coronation of Queen Elizabeth II in 1953. Huge numbers in the country got their first TV set for this momentous occasion. There must have been 20 people crammed into that tiny 12x12 living room to see the procession and ceremony. Everyone was awestruck, reverently quiet as if we were in the Abbey with everybody. It was so kind of the Haywood family to be invaded like they were and have us all in to see it. When the Luke family, US, finally got a television, it stood in the front room festooned with aluminum foil attached to the rabbit ears that were perched on top of the set to act as an aerial. It was 12x12, black and white, and we tended to approach it very gingerly as if it might do something unexpected any minute. We would turn it on and all sit gazing at snow interference, zigzag lines, or an image bisected completely and only partly the right way up. My father, of course, considered himself the keeper of this Holy Grail and claimed authority to be the only one to touch it. He would fiddle and fuss, moving the rabbit ears about, attaching bits of foil here and there, all to no avail.

Losing patience, he would say, "That's it. Trouble is at t'other end", meaning it wasn't the set or him, but trouble at the BBC at the other end of things. My younger brother Graham was dying to get in there and fix it, of course, he knew how to, but NO..." It's "t'other end," and that was final. So my father decamped to the pub, the King Bill, short for King William IV, and the minute his footsteps had faded away, up jumped Graham (nine years old at the time), and he promptly fixed it with no trouble. We would settle down happily to watch. As I remember, it always seemed to be Muffin the Mule or The Flowerpot Men. We didn't care; the miracle of the whole thing had us in thrall! My father would arrive home later from the pub and bang through the vestibule door to find us all watching the excellent picture. "I TOLD you so, "he proclaimed," trouble was at t'other end." The three of us studiously avoided looking at each other, and off he went none the wiser. This phrase "It's t'other end" became something we would say throughout the years if something was wrong and causing a problem; it was "at t'other end! It always makes us laugh.

Later on, when we had moved away and were paying a visit back home, my husband and I were on a bus to Preston, and it went through Chorley. The bus made many stops, and one was right in front of a row house, but this particular one was certainly different. The window was crammed with Elvis paraphernalia! A lady sitting next to us, headscarf, basket and all, noticed us looking at it. It was so incongruous in the middle of Chorley, especially as there was a huge sign in the middle proclaiming that this small residence was the Headquarters of the Elvis Presley Fan Club Chorley Branch. "Oh aye," said the lady, "the feller who lives in there is mad about Elvis. He goes around dressed up as Elvis, and if anybody notices and sez owt, "is 'ed guz up!" We were totally diverted and sorry he wasn't catching our bus that day, so we could have seen him in all his finery and watched " 'is 'ed go up !"

I mustn't forget the New Year's Day Fair. Every year caravans and lorries would arrive in town and set up near the bus station. Back then, it might have been on land that became the bus station, near the Outdoor Market. The Fair had Waltzers, Carrousels with horses going up and down, Dodgers, The Caterpillar, and many other rather dilapidated rides. There were umpteen things to test your skill; throwing hoops, darts, swinging hammers, and so on. I always hurried past the Freak Show. It seems unthinkable now in more politically correct times, but it was the big draw. Usually, a bearded lady would be outside in some spangly outfit, looking thoroughly exhausted, and beside her, the Barker would be hollering in a booming voice about the freakish wonders within. Many foods were on offer, but the only thing we ever got was a cup of black peas in a small round pot container with a small spoon. You stepped behind the huge simmering pot of peas and sat on one of the three or four ancient wooden benches lining the tent. These objects looked like they had been traveling the highways and byways since medieval times. My father took me every year to this Fair, and it was a much-anticipated event. It was run down and shabby, but the bright lights, profusion of sequins, and splashes of color gave the whole fair an exciting and magical atmosphere.

I haven't said much about the Radio and its place in our lives. It was so important and brought the outside world into our kitchen. The house in Richelieu Street had two rooms downstairs about 12x12, the front room, which rarely got used, and the kitchen that had a table, four assorted chairs, a clothes maiden, and a wooden frame on ropes that hung in the air, usually draped with washing trying its best to dry. There was a small fireplace that needed black leading, and it had a hob on which a kettle sat that was nearly always on the boil. We drank a lot of tea, and at moments of crisis, or for any reason at all, someone would say, let's have a cup of tea. So it was good to have the kettle simmering there. The Dolly Tub stood in a corner with the washing board and other items for washing clothes each Monday. There was a kitchenette piece of furniture that had cupboards and shelves, but not very many, and of course, there was the kitchen sink. Later, a gas stove arrived, and my mother made great use of that. You can imagine that when we were all in there, it was pretty crowded. Pride of place on the kitchen table was the radio. It was old and very battered, but it worked. I do remember us in wartime listening intently, the pip pip pip noise followed by "This is the BBC News" in a serious upper-class voice. We would sit riveted to news of the events unfolding, none of them good. I remember us listening grimly to Winston Churchill and his stirring words. I read them now, and I am amazed at how great he was. We would eat our main meal in the middle of the day (this being the North of England, it was called dinner), and in the late afternoon, we would have " our tea, "which was a small meal. None of the meals were very big, and I was always hungry, as most of us were in those days. The radio would be on as we ate, and Workers Playtime would be broadcast at noon. This was a show to boost morale amongst workers in different factories around the country. I remember hearing Julie Andrews as a very young girl about 12 years old or so, performing with her parents and singing like an angel. Sometimes Dame Myra Hess would play the piano, and lovely haunting Chopin struck a beautiful chord in a complex world. Who could forget Arthur Askey and Mrs. Mop with her saucy question, " Can I do you now sir?" George Formby with his ukelele, Gracie Fields, known to all as "Our Gracie," and the incomparable Vera Lynn. So many other acts and all were boisterously received by the workers and appreciated by a vast radio audience.

We loved Dick Barton, who was on in the early evening; he was a detective. I can still hear that introductory music now. We hated to miss this 15-minute ongoing drama. Children's Hour was on in the afternoon, also Woman's Hour, and of course, Mrs. Dale's Diary. In the evenings, there would be serials acted out in six or seven episodes. I couldn't get enough of those. Later would come The Archers, a soap opera about a farming family, which still goes on today. The BBC played a lot of classical music, and I would have this station on during my ballet phase when I danced and danced in the Front Room. Ah yes, the radio, it was terrific entertainment. The weather forecasts were constant, of course. It's one thing we aren't short of in England, the weather. Just where are Heligoland, Dogger Bank, and all the other mysterious places that the solemn voiced announcer would pontificate about? Gale force winds were often a standard feature, of course!

We went through a phase when Pen Pals became a big thing. Maybe it started in the war or something, but suddenly everyone seemed to be getting an American pen pal. Mine was named Lillian and lived in Pennsylvania. I think one of the teachers gave out the names and addresses. Lillian's letters told me of cars, boyfriends, the Prom. The Prom? She would send me pictures of her in her "Prom dress," and to me, looking at this, it seemed like I was in touch with someone who lived on another planet. Her life experience was so far from mine. It seemed like another world which it was. Now I am an American and proud of it, but it was unbelievable and like a fantasyland to think about back then. I had never been in a car, and here was Lillian driving one that had been given to her as a gift! I wish I had kept in touch, but the correspondence dwindled. No doubt she found my life equally strange.

In my early years, shopping was different. At the end of some streets would be a corner shop stocking a little bit of everything. Bread and milk were always available but a little higher in price to make up for the convenience. A ham slicer usually had pride of place to sell boiled ham. Usually, a quarter of a pound would do for our tea with lettuce and other homegrown things, and that was for four of us! A slightly longer walk in any direction would bring us to a more significant road, in our case Rishton Lane, and there were more shops on either side of this particular stretch, forming quite a good little selection of shops. There was the butcher, chemist, greengrocer, fishmonger, confectionery, and so on. The shops were small. The butcher's shop had two men in there wearing blood-stained aprons, wielding large cleavers as they stood ready to cut you the piece of meat you wanted if it wasn't already on display in the window. Lamb was plentiful and cheaper then, unlike now when one needs a second mortgage to buy a joint of lamb. Often a pig's head adorned the window display, usually wearing a natty straw hat. It presided over the white enamel trays that contained tripe (of course), black puddings, sausages in long links, and other meats. One of my earliest memories is of me as a baby, sitting in my large pram outside the butcher's shop, probably nine months old. I could see my mother inside. I was screaming my head off, feeling abandoned. This is a fleeting memory, but still there. If I could only remember where I put the car keys when lost with the same recall, it would be really good! When I grew older, I was often sent up to the butchers for a quarter pound of minced meat (hamburger to Americans.) My Mother could work miracles with a quarter pound of this meat. She would always send me off saying, "Watch your change and ask him for a pig's trotter and tell him to leave the leg on."

The Chemist's Shop window had two large vaguely Arabian-shaped glass vials filled with colored liquid, red and green. It was a small shop that sold a few over-the-counter medicines and toiletries, always fascinating. On the shelves at the back were small drawers for all the ingredients for the potions on hand. You would tell the chemist what ailed you, and he would make up a remedy for you, either in a small package or in a bottle. Mysterious mixtures but intensely believed in. There were always many tonics for the ever-present malady in Lancashire, which was in those days, NERVES. This all-encompassing word covered the spectrum of depression, anxiety, worry, hysteria, hypochondria, idleness, you name it, and NERVES covered it. It was like an epidemic! Sometimes it seemed you heard more about nerves than you wished to.

The Confectioners sold terrific bread and cakes. You could smell it on your way to the shops, just a great whiff of baking and goodies. On sale were bread, flour cakes, small cakes, iced buns, iced slices a la Napoleon, tea cakes, Victoria sponges, Dundee cake, cream slices, gingerbread, and I could go on and on. In my mind, the pies and pasties were the crowning jewels in this collection. I remember days long before curries and other international dishes were available everywhere.

The Dress Shop always had an elegant display window and prices way above our pay grade. I mustn't forget the ever-present Fish and Chip Shop and an Ironmonger. Mothers shopped every day for the main meal as no one we knew had a refrigerator. Weekly, my mother and I walked to the Town Center, to explore and enjoy the larger shops of all kinds that were available. Thorntons Toffee Shop was one of our favorites and is still going today, and things taste just as good.

Today, shopping is totally different, but in those earlier years, we counted it a blessing that we had things available. After the severe shortages during the war, we were grateful to get anything. I forget how things have changed!

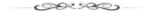

Chapter Seventeen

LAST THOUGHTS

When I set out to write this, my wish was to recover and write down memories, mainly of the second world war, for my grandchildren. The writing was extended as memories began to come back and flood me, and writing them down was easy and satisfying. My childhood wasn't easy, but I survived, mainly because of a wonderful mother. I would often sit outside on the front step with Bruce the neighbor's dog, a particular friend of mine. I would have my arm around his wooly coat, and inside me, a voice said over and over, "I will leave here." I always had a resolve that I would leave and go abroad when the time came. I know now that geography isn't the answer to inner struggles, but the move when it came did get me started on a life journey that took me away from my roots and brought me untold life experiences and so many blessings.

- 135 -

So remembering Lancashire as it was for me brought things full circle somehow. Someone once told me that the secret to a happy life is 98 percent perspective. As I walked down Memory Lane back to Lancashire as I knew it, I developed a different perspective on it all. It's no longer a place I wanted to leave but a place I now treasure. I can see and appreciate how many gifts and opportunities it gave me. I'm grateful for them all.

Lancashire is a beautiful county with a proud history, and I am so glad I was part of it. Life was hard for so many through the generations, but their struggles to survive gave toughness and resilience to the people. Though it falters sometimes, some of that is in me and mine, and I am glad of it. The people didn't only survive; they built a society full of variety, humor, caring, music, standards to live by, hard work, and so much more. They developed a stubborn resolve never to give up and to work hard for a better future for themselves and those who came after them. I am proud my roots are in Lancashire. Though Bolton was a Puritan stronghold in the English Civil War, it was also a hidden stronghold for the Catholic Faith throughout the hundreds of years of oppression. I marvel at the Lancashire Martyrs who died for their faith. When I was 40, I entered the Catholic church and felt I had come home. I had thought my Anglican parents would be unhappy, but my Father peacefully said, "It's in the blood," and that was that. I developed an awareness and new respect for the faithfulness of the Catholic people in the area. I am proud of the Cotton Mill Workers who, despite their hardships, supported Gandhi and the Indian people who began to make their own cotton. There is a picture of Gandhi visiting the Lancashire Mill Workers after Indian Independence, thanking them for their sacrifices and support.

I always try to remember that it's good to stroll down Memory Lane sometimes, but never good to build a house down there and move in and wallow. This stroll down the lane proved to be enjoyable and healing. Walking back up and out of the memories, I find I have a profound thankfulness for my experiences and my Lancashire background. I was, and continue to be, blessed by it.

THE LANCASHIRE ROSE

ABOUT THE AUTHOR

was born in Bolton Lancashire in 1937. I lived through the Second World War, went to college in London, lived and taught in Enfield, Essex for a year, and then married my husband in August 1958. In 1959, we moved to Jamaica, West Indies, where my two precious daughters were born. In1964, we returned to England for three years in the Bristol, Somerset area, and loved that beautiful part of the world. In 1967 we moved to St Croix, U.S. Virgin Islands. We lived there for 17 years and the island will forever have a treasured place in our hearts. Every year we lived in the Caribbean we returned to England in the summer to see our parents. We kept up with our roots in Lancashire on these visits. I had a career in education until we moved to the United States in 1984 and lived for two years in Alvin, Texas. We made many friends who took us to their hearts and made us part of the family. We loved the Lone Star State, but in late 1986 we moved to Fredericksburg Virginia to be near to our two daughters who were both in the North East. We found a home and have been here for just over30 years. The geographical journey of my life was the setting for my spiritual journey. It began in Bolton, Lancashire, and brought me to Virginia. I sit on my rocker on my front porch and remember Lancashire with fondness now. Writing all these memories was a good experience. Now I am 85, retired, and dealing with the pandemic like everyone else! Life has its twists and turns! I hope you enjoyed your taste of Lancashire.

Made in the USA
Middletown, DE
13 March 2022

62602052R00086